To Marilyn Casper -
You
give
me !
hope
Bob Pesko
3-19-86

SHOW ME NO MERCY

A Compelling Story of Remarkable Courage

Robert Perske

Abingdon Press / Nashville

SHOW ME NO MERCY:
A Compelling Story of Remarkable Courage

Copyright © 1984 by Robert Perske

Third Printing 1984

Library of Congress Cataloging in Publication Data

PERSKE, ROBERT.
  Show me no mercy.
  Summary: Paralyzed in an accident that kills his wife and
daughter, Andy Banks, a bus driver, struggles to overcome his
handicap and to keep his teenage son with Down's Syndrome
from being institutionalized.
  [1. Fathers and sons—Fiction. 2. Down's syndrome—
Fiction. 3. Physically handicapped—Fiction.
4. Handicapped—Fiction] I. Title.
PZ7.P437Sh   1984   [Fic]   83-21384

ISBN 0-687-38435-4

Manufactured by the Parthenon Press
Nashville, Tennessee, United States of America

For
    Martha,
    Ann,
    Dawn,
    Lee,
    Marc,
    Richard,
    and Tony

1 "MOVE THAT RAKE!" I said.

"Mmmove yer own," Ben said.

Working side by side, my son and I stroked red, gold, and brown leaves into a long line, uncovering the grass in our backyard.

"Nice day," I said.

"Yep," Ben said.

"Makes a guy glad he's living in Seahaven."

"Yep."

It was the Saturday before Thanksgiving. A warm breeze off the Atlantic pushed the clouds inland, permitting the 22,000 citizens of our New England town to enjoy the sunshiny 62 degrees.

I raked faster.

Ben did, too.

"Think you can keep up with me?" I asked.

"Yep."

"Don't want a sissy working with me."

"Yyyer the sissy."

Our rakes flashed as if they were attached to engines going full throttle. We raced until my lungs ached and sweat ran off my forehead, burning my eyes. A quick glance at those stubby, muscular arms of my five-foot-five kid, who showed no sign of letting up, sent my mind flashing back to that maternity ward sixteen years earlier. "See that muscle tone," the doctor had said, pointing to infant Ben's arms. "He'll never be strong."

Aching muscles snapped me out of the past and screamed at me to stop this craziness immediately and rest. But how could I, and still save face?

I dropped my rake, snatched some leaves, and threw them at Ben. He snatched a handful and let me have it in the face. I sputtered, shook the leaves out of my hair, picked up a trash can full of leaves, and emptied it over his head. Ben came at me like a bowling ball, tackled me in the midsection, and shoved me back into a high pile we had made earlier.

"Mom! *Mom!* They're at it again." Beth, Ben's twin sister, was shouting from a bedroom window. "Make them stop. Everybody'll think they're crazy!"

"Aw, c'mon, Andy!" my wife yelled through the screen door. "Stop it right now! The neighbors will think you're killing each other!"

"You got it, Maggie. This boy has gone too far. Might as well call the undertaker."

"Gabloney!" Ben said. *"Yyer* under *me."*

Tillie, our little Pekingese, pushed her flat face against the screen. Then she barked furiously, scolding us for leaving her out of the fun.

Our next-door neighbor on the east, an elderly widow named Beatrice Peck, looked out her back door to see what was going on. When she saw Ben and me, she withdrew and slammed the door.

"See!" Maggie said. "I told you."

"Aw, she already thinks we're weird," I said.

The grinning faces of the O'Briens, Big Richard and Joanne, suddenly appeared above our fence on the west—the one that divided our property from theirs.

"Big Rich," Maggie called, "make them stop."

"You kiddin'?" the burly giant truck driver said. "I just bet Joanne ten bucks the kid'll do the old man in."

"You're a heckuva neighbor!" Maggie said.

I bridged up, turned quickly, got a hammer-lock on Ben's head and rolled him over, with me on top. "Give?" I said.

Ben snickered. "I never give up."

He never did. And what's more, his well-practiced "I-never-give-ups" were spoken clearly. And yet the doctor had pointed at newborn Ben's tongue and declared he'd never speak understandably.

Of course, Ben did have a speech problem. Although he knew exactly what he wanted to say, some syllables came out as if he had to unglue them from his tongue while others were expelled in tiny rapid explosions. And sometimes they came out in the wrong order. Even so, the doctor was wrong; we understood our son—sometimes too well.

Ben squirmed. I grabbed both his shoulders and shoved down hard, pushing my face down, too, until my nose touched his. Ben relaxed and grinned impishly.

How I loved that face! I had loved it even when the doctor called my attention to the epicanthal folds on Ben's eyes, told us "sympathetically" that our baby had Down's Syndrome and that we didn't have to take him home. I had loved that little face with the oriental eyes enough to get another doctor on the case before the sun had set.

And that tiny, wiry Maggie—God bless Maggie. She loved that face, too. She had loved it so much that when sad-looking visitors dropped in, she pepped them up and sent them away smiling. She even held Aunt Phoebe Paxton, our only relative on the East Coast, at bay when Phoebe had suggested that we "keep the sweet little girl and send the tragedy away." And when that oldest, most-powerful sister of Maggie's mother did not let up, my wife had folded her arms, set her jaw, and looked straight into Aunt Phoebe's eyes. Maggie became an immovable object, and I swear, she would have stayed that way for hours if I hadn't exploded and told Phoebe to get out of the room.

All the pressures from outsiders that were meant to divide our family only brought us closer. But some nights, Maggie and I had wrapped ourselves around each other in bed and cried ourselves to sleep.

A handful of leaves jammed into my face jarred me back to the present again. As I spit out bits and pieces, Ben wriggled free and slapped a half nelson on me, spinning me over until both my shoulder blades touched the ground.

I strained to free myself until my lungs felt as if they'd burst. Of course, if I had been angry, I'd have gotten loose all right. But being only slightly taller than Ben and in my late forties, with my energy fading and his coming on stronger, it wasn't clear how much I would be faking it if I let him win.

The screen door burst open and a five-pound ball of reddish-brown fur soared off the back step, hit the ground with feet churning, and streaked toward us. Then she was all over us, growling and licking and making us laugh. When we stopped, she plopped down on the grass, flat from tail to chin and, with brown eyes too big for her face, watched, daring us to move.

"Better give," Ben said. "No mmmercy."

"No mercy? First you use all my wrestling holds against me. Now it's my own words?"

"Yep. No mmercy."

"Well, if you have to, say it right. Say it like this: 'No mercy.' "

"No mercy!"

"Perfect! You've got me. I'm a goner now."

"I wwon't hurt," Ben said. "Just fun."

"Andy," Maggie urged, "get up. Ben's got to be at the diner in an hour."

"Right, Mag," I said. "Let's get movin', Ben."

Ben let out a contented giggle. "Give up first."

"Look, you stubborn kid. I still have my secret weapon."

"Not fair. Tickllling's dirty."

"Oh, all right. I give up."

"C'mon, Joanne," Big Rich said. "Told ya those Greyhound Bus drivers don't have what it takes." The two faces disappeared.

We brushed ourselves off and started to rake again.

When all the leaves were layered in our compost enclosure, six inches of leaves to an inch of dirt, Ben put in a bucket of worms to help things along. As the squirmers wriggled

12

themselves into their leafy hotel, Ben, with the air of a gracious manager, told them to enjoy their stay—eat like kings.

He was a kind hotelier. When a wet snow or heavy rain drove worms out of the earth, he picked up the stranded wayfarers and placed them snugly in the heap. There was always room at his inn.

Ben and I were putting away the rakes and trash can when Beth came out, followed by Maggie. Beth stopped and put an arm around me.

Ben and Beth—what a combination! Beth had come into the world thirty-six minutes after Ben (a fact he never lets her forget). They were the same height and had my brown hair, but both possessed Maggie's eyes, as warm and brown as the shell of a hazelnut. And they could purse their lips tightly and smile like devilish pixies, just as Maggie did.

Of course, when they became angry their lips pushed together tightly, too, but you could sure tell the difference. They had their mother's high cheekbones, inherited from a distant Apache ancestor, and all three had a look of quiet determination and direction.

And yet Beth was reading street signs and billboards when she was three, while Ben was still struggling to say single words plainly. Beth soared ahead, becoming sharper than her parents at computing, grasping textbook concepts, and passing academic tests. Her twin had to work at learning like a bird with short wings.

But Ben had no match among us in other areas. When the four of us went to pick out a Pekingese puppy from a litter of six, Ben took over, insisting we choose the sickly runt because that little girl needed all the help she could get.

"Guess what?" Beth asked.

"Don't know what," I said, "but from the look on your face, it's got to be big."

She wrapped her arms around my neck and squeezed. "Matt O'Brien invited me to a movie tonight."

For a moment, I was at a loss for words, but Ben filled the silence. "Mmatt O'Brien! Really?"

"Right, Ben," Beth answered.

I gave Maggie a quizzical glance, asking with my eyes whether trouble was brewing. Maggie wrinkled her nose, clasped her hands in front, and gave me her tight-lipped smile, letting me know she thought it was okay.

"Well, well," I said. "Is this that 210-pound blond hulk next door, Seahaven High's all-star fullback—the one Ben's always hounding?"

"Yep," Ben said.

"Is this the guy to whom my willowy sophomore-cheerleader daughter screams words

of praise, even though he dates only highfalu-
tin seniors?"

"Hush, Dad," Beth said. "He'll hear you.
Just say I can go."

"You can't go."

Still hanging on my neck, Beth leaned back
and looked at me. Seeing a smile, she planted a
wet kiss on my cheek.

"Have a good time, honey," I said.

Beth had started for the house when Ben
asked, "Dad, can I take a brreak at the diner?
Come home? Say hi when Mmatt comes?"

Beth turned and looked at me, her smile
gone, anger showing in her eyes.

I hoped I was the only one who noticed.

"No, Ben," I said. "Stay at work. No mercy."

2   THE NEXT DAY, Sunday, I was up by 6:00. After greeting sunrises almost every morning for 18 years while cruising down Interstate 95 in the driver's seat of a Greyhound Americruiser, I found it impossible to sleep in on my days off. I headed for the kitchen and rummaged for the coffeepot and skillet.

"Morning, Dad." Beth appeared in the doorway in her pajamas and housecoat.

"What are you doing up?" I asked.

"Heard you."

"Didn't think I made that much noise. Have some breakfast with me."

After finishing off a cheese-and-onion omelette and more home-fried potatoes than we needed, we sat at the table—I sipped a cup of coffee and Beth, her cocoa.

"You saw, didn't you, Dad?"

"Saw what?"

"Yesterday when Ben asked to be home when Matt came, you saw me . . . "

"Wait a minute, honey; we can talk about sister-brother complications later. Tell me about last night."

A smile appeared and her eyes sparkled.

"That good, huh?"

"He was nice. And the movie was great!"

"The guy's got good taste. But what about all those childhood hassles—teasing, throwing things, bawling, and running to mothers? And during junior high, each of you acted as if the other had a stench!"

"He's changed."

"So have you."

Beth studied her cocoa for awhile. "There's more, Dad."

"No!" I said, holding up my palms. "My heart won't take anymore."

"You big clown! Stop it."

"Okay."

"Matt told me he's trying out for basketball manager tomorrow after school. Our cheerleading practice is at the same time at the other end of the gym. Matt asked to walk home with me."

"Oh-oh," I said. "I'm stopping this right now or we'll have a marriage by next Saturday. O'Brien in-laws! That oversized prank-pulling trucker, always blasting me with his air horn when he passes me on I-95; that woman who's always trying to make us eat enough food for an army; and a son-in-law who's a jock!"

"You said you'd stop clowning!"

We sat quietly for a few minutes; then I started again. "How come Matt's going out for manager?"

"He's never been as good at basketball as football. He wants to study coaching next year at college, and he thinks the managing experience could help. Coach Rossi said he was welcome to try out."

I told Beth it sounded like a wise move.

We sat quietly and studied our cups again. Then I decided to face the issue head on.

"Tell you what, kid," I said. "Let's go back and talk about what you think I saw when—"

Ben walked in, rubbing his eyes.

"You're late, Ben," I said. "Sun's been up an hour. You losing your touch?"

"Nope. Lisstening to CB."

"Anything doin'?"

"Nnnot much. Just truckers. Talkin'."

Ben stood behind Beth's chair and massaged her shoulders.

"That feels good, Ben," she said. "Go a little lower . . . Now to the left."

"There?"

"Ohh yes! Right there. You're the best back massager in the whole world."

"Yep. I'm the best."

I watched them, feeling a fatherly pride. But I also felt a sadness.

3   I DIDN'T HAVE another chance to be alone with Beth until around 1:00 that afternoon. Then Ben took off for a swim in the public indoor pool with his pals from the special-education class—Sarah Rooney and Josh Huff, who also had Down's Syndrome. Maggie and the other two moms went along to chat and watch.

"Beth," I began, "want to finish our talk now?"

"I want to, Dad, but Heather Pendleton and I have a chemistry assignment. Her dad said he'd help us develop a computer program for determining the atomic weight of things."

"That's nice," I said. "Let me know when you and Heather need help determining how to double-clutch and downshift a 49-passenger cross-country bus on a steep hill."

Beth gave me a sharp look, then a smile. "You're jealous."

"Naa! Well, honey, maybe a little. Lots of brilliant pops in this town—professors like Heather Pendleton's dad."

"Look, Dad. Dr. Pendleton may be a math wizard, but he's a jumpy guy. It'll be a miracle if he and Heather can spend the afternoon together without fighting. Last week they argued over transferring her to a private school in Vermont."

"You mean one of those places they used to call finishing schools?"

"Uh-huh. She said she'd run away first. And you know what she told me? She said she wished she lived with *us*."

"She said that?"

"That's right. Uhh, Dad . . . I probably won't be back until 10:30. You're on the early morning run; you'll be in bed. Talk tomorrow?"

"Sure, kid. Tomorrow."

As the door closed, I sat back in my easy chair, locked my fingers behind my head, and relaxed. Then I began thinking about those "finishing schools." What did they mean by that? Did parents really believe children could become . . . well, finished persons? Complete editions? Perfect products?

***

"Let's go, Tillie," I said. "It's 9:00. Time for our Sunday evening rounds."

Tillie dashed for the front door and waited till I joined her. Then we headed east on Bannister Street, Tillie taking twenty little plinks for one of my strides. We walked the eight blocks to the high school, two more to the town square. Crossing the square, we continued on Bannister over Interstate 95 and the New York-to-Boston railroad tracks, then six more blocks to our favorite rock on the beach. Tillie went sniffing around while I studied the lights at sea.

Then we headed for Kowalski's Diner on the east side of the square.

At the entrance, I took a leash from my pocket and tethered Tillie to the wrought-iron railing. "Not fair, making you a second-class citizen, but it's the law."

Tillie barked three piercing pleas as I went inside. I found only Barney up front, cleaning the grill. We said hi, then I asked if he had chased all his customers away.

"Naw. It's always this way before Thanksgiving."

"Hey, Ben," Barney called toward the back room. "Your dad's here. You serve him."

A grinning Ben appeared, took off his soiled apron, put on a clean one, washed his hands, and placed himself in front of me, both palms on the counter. "What you have, ssir?"

"I'll have the marinated hasenpfeffer dinner, a bowl of escargot bisque and a Peach Perfection tart."

Ben stifled a laugh, rolled his eyes, and shifted his weight to one foot. "Don't be a smmart ask."

I chuckled at how dangerously close to profanity Ben came. Somehow he'd learned

23

that unabashed profanity—like that used by many of us—could be the straw that kept some folks from liking him.

"Okay, make it apple pie and coffee and a snack for the lady outside."

"Comin' up," Ben tried to sound exactly like Barney. He served me and then stood like a soldier at attention.

"You like watching me eat?"

"Yep."

"Work's done?"

"Yep."

"All the pots and pans? Dishes? Floor scrubbed?"

Barney suddenly threw down his grill rag, turned, and placed his short barrel-chested body in front of me, palms on the counter. "Get off my employee's back, will ya?"

Ben snickered, headed for the other end of the counter, and began to wipe vigorously. Our eyes followed him.

"The guy sure knows how to work, Andy."

"Yeah, thanks to you and Polly Patterson."

"I guess. By the way, I miss seeing that feisty teacher around here. When Ben was a question mark, she was here a lot."

"She did spice up the place."

"Sure did. The only teacher I ever knew who'd put on an apron and work side by side with her student. And the way that tall, skinny, long-legged lady bounced in here three months ago, ordering me to hire Ben and promising I'd never be sorry!"

"The part I remember best came after all of us were sure Ben would make it. She planted a kiss on you and said she'd marry you if you bought a stool to stand on and dyed the grey hair sticking out of your shirt."

"Crazy kid. And me old enough to be her father. Anyway . . . tell her to come around more often."

"Okay, Barney."

Tillie shattered the silence that followed with a rapid fire of angry barks. Then Officer Harry Brill charged into the diner and headed straight for Ben. "All right, kid. I wanna know right now! Did that dog get its rabies shot?"

Ben tried to kick out the right words, but Brill's attack closed his sending system down like a pinball machine gone *TILT*. And to make matters worse, he was trying to compensate for his muteness by standing with feet apart, hands on hips, staring at the officer. He looked like a baby chick in front of a cobra, but this cop of the old school interpreted it as raw defiance.

"The dog's had rabies shots," I said, as Brill prepared to step up his attack.

Brill whirled. "Oh! . . . Didn't see ya there.

. . . Just needed to check. . . . Reached down to pet it and it bit me. . . . Uhh . . . Sure is a cute little bugger. Barney, give me a coffee. Black."

Ben hurried into the back room.

I sat there quietly, thinking that someday I might kill that officious cop. Our town had one of the finest police departments on the East Coast, and all the officers understood the kids in special education—except for Brill. We in Polly Patterson's special-ed parent group had passed around, by the grapevine, the names of those doctors, dentists, shopkeepers, and others whom our children should avoid. The only cop on that list was Brill, and he was up near the top.

Harry Brill—still walking the town beat in his late fifties while younger officers were promoted to sergeant, captain, and higher. Nevertheless, he presented an imposing facade—a tall, never-in-doubt career policeman, striding around head held high, as if he were receiving special instructions from the FBI through extrasensory perception. But if you looked closely, you could distinguish the mouth of a bully and the eyes of a coward.

A year ago, Brill had grabbed Ben's classmate little Josh Huff and hauled him in for writing a "dirty phrase" on Sholer's Department Store wall with spray paint. A bunch of us from the parent group had gone down to the police station and testified that Josh could never have written *AD ASTRA PER ASPERA*. When the co-president of our parent group, Dr. Manfred Rooney, said that the Latin phrase meant "to the stars through difficulty," the Huffs had told the desk sergeant they wished to heck Josh *had* been guilty!

Brill leaned over his cup as if nothing had happened. Barney went back to cleaning the grill, attacking it as if he'd like to scrub away the mean streak in his unwanted customer. Then he went into the back room and told Ben to take off early; he'd lock up.

Ben came back, still looking scared, and we left.

After I unhooked Tillie, she leaped high enough for Ben to scoop her up in his arms. He held her close and let her lick his face.

"It's okay," he said. "You're ssafe now. It's okay, Tillie."

He set her down and fed her some bits of hamburger. She sauntered to the curb, turned and waited for a signal.

Ben looked both ways for cars. "Let's go, Tillie."

She leaped off the curb and crossed the street like a ball bouncing over words in a sing-along movie, landing in her most graceful arc on the opposite curb. When her feet touched the grass, she sped toward the war memorial statue in the middle of the square. There she turned around, bellied-down on the lawn, and waited for Ben and me.

Ben stared up at the statue as if he were looking at God. On the pedestal stood the figure of a U.S. Navy enlisted man, feet apart and hands on hips. His hat was cocked toward the right brow. Wearing a faint smile, the statue seemed to be looking at something far out on the water.

My "concrete thinking" son, always struggling to get solid handles on life and tucking them into repetitive rituals, led me in the 9,982nd discussion of Machinist's Mate Third Class James Franklin Bannister, born October 16, 1923, in Seahaven and killed on the *U.S.S. Arizona* at Pearl Harbor on December 7, 1941. We talked about Bannister, who had pulled three buddies out of the burning engine room to safety. When he went down for the fourth, he had not returned.

Ben reached down and touched the last words one by one as he recited them flawlessly:

ALTHOUGH THE ENEMY SHOWED NO MERCY
HE DID NOT GIVE UP. ERECTED BY THE
CITIZENS OF SEAHAVEN, DECEMBER 7, 1946

Ben turned toward the sea, with feet apart and hands on hips like Bannister, just as he had while facing Brill. When he was a child Ben had mouthed the phrases, making us laugh. But recently when he paid tribute to the hero, his eyes looked as though he were arming to fight countless battles, all alone. I began to feel an uneasiness about this ritual and wished we could do something else. But I didn't know how to tell Ben.

As the three of us headed home, I wondered if the stuff about never giving up that I had put into my son's head might someday lead to disaster. Other parents of teenagers in Polly Patterson's class seemed . . . well, less intense about achievement. Of course, the Rooneys (Manfred and Sally, professors of psychology and English, respectively, at Oceanside College and co-presidents of our parent group) did develop magic tricks, counting and spelling games for Sarah. And Auggy Huff, a carpenter, was always building scooters and things out of wood for Josh. But they never raised things to such a do-or-die pitch, like I did.

I was a bus driver, darn it, raised on a diet of wrestling holds and heroes by tough brothers on a farm outside Omaha, Nebraska. So I gave Ben what I knew.

God knows, I wanted more than anything for Ben to grow up and make it in the world on his own. But as his adulthood approached, I worried. Was I right, trying to harden Ben? Or was I preparing him to walk into a buzz saw?

"There's your classroom," I said as we passed a portable annex outside Seahaven High School.

"Mmain building's better."

"It beats going miles to classes in rented church basements like you used to. Be satisfied."

"Can't."

"Stubborn guy. If I know you, you'll be Mr. Charmball, trying to work yourself in with the regulars."

"Yep. Soon."

"What do you mean by that?"

"Bbbbasketball tryouts. Monday, after school."

"How'd you learn about that?"

"Announcement. P.A. system."

"Think you're a basketball player?"

"Nope. . . . Mmmanager."

"Hey, Ben. You may be walking into trouble. Lots of competition."

"Maybe. Gotta try."

I felt a sinking in my stomach. Ben would be going up against Matt. For years I'd watched that neighbor kid go after challenges, always coming out on top. And now Ben had decided to go for a slot with the "regulars," not knowing yet that he'd have to beat out a guy who was *more* than regular.

My conscience screamed at me that this was all my fault. I was the one who had put all those charge-ahead ideas into my kid's head.

And yet Ben had drive and spirit, too. Maybe more. Just because my son had one lousy extra chromosome—that blasted Trisomy 21—life for him had become an obstacle course. And as if that weren't enough, experts had labeled him with the name of a dead doctor. How I hated the words *Down's Syndrome!* And others, picking up on the label, had kept him out of many regular teenage activities he longed to be in. They ignored him or shoved him back or pitied him or stared at him or snickered at him—often making him feel ashamed, as if it were *his* fault!

And yet Ben still refused to see himself as a tragedy. He refused, even when it was mirrored in the faces of really strange people like Phoebe and Brill and that jumpy neighbor Mrs. Peck, who backpedaled into her house every time Ben offered her tomatoes from our garden.

And Matt, the hometown hero. Well, he was a good kid. But when everybody talked about the courage of Seahaven High's fullback, it got to me sometimes. He was only living up to his potential. If they wanted to see a guy with *real* courage, they should have been watching Ben.

Matt always accomplished things with ease, while Ben had to struggle for everything he got in life. Since the day he was born, the guy would grit his teeth and sweat and get knocked down and get up again and sweat some more—and do things some experts swore he'd never do. And who cheered *him* on as a hero?

Of course, Maggie and I thought Big Rich and Joanne were great for training Matt to be kind and to do things with Ben every once in awhile. (That made Ben worship Matt as if he were a god.) But I felt a little bitter sometimes when I noticed how smoothly he ditched Ben when some of the other letter-jacketed heroes came around. Now that he was interested in Beth, would he have her shying away from Ben, too?

It suddenly hit me that I'd been so preoccupied with my own thoughts that I had walked five blocks without a word to Ben. I tried to calm down.

But even then unsolved dilemmas loomed large in my mind. Should I wait up and tell Beth about Ben's plan? Should I talk to Matt? Or should I just let it ride? And—the most painful question of all—had I, in my pushy way, set Ben up for a terrible fall?

"You'll be proud of me sommeday, Dad," Ben said.

"Hey, Ben, I'm proud of you now!"

4   MONDAY WAS ROUGH. Getting passengers safely to their destinations up and down I-95 is bad enough on a good day. But it's hell when a guy hasn't had a good night's sleep. I breathed a sigh of relief as I walked in the back door at suppertime.

"Hi, everybody. I'm home," I shouted, closing the door behind me.

No answer.

Then a commotion erupted at the other end of the house and Tillie sped through the kitchen doorway, zigzagging for joy toward me.

"Hi, Tillie." I picked her up and hugged her and got two licks on the cheek before I put her down.

I glanced at a note from Maggie. She and Sally Rooney were at Seahaven Hospital, visiting a Mrs. Matlock who had a newborn child with Down's Syndrome. The note also instructed me to set the oven at 325° and do something to a casserole dish in the refrigerator. It ended with large printed letters: I WILL MURDER YOU IF YOU DO NOT DO THESE THINGS AS SOON AS YOU COME IN!

"Getcha in a minute," I said to the oven as I draped my jacket over a chair, opened the refrigerator, took out an ice-cold beer and a piece of longhorn cheese, and headed for the living room.

I settled into the recliner, leaned back, let my legs rise, and enjoyed my first easy moment of the day.

Tillie leaped onto my lap and stared at the cheese. I gave her a piece and was preparing to take my first sip of cold beer when the front door opened and Ben and Beth appeared. Ben walked toward me, taking his long strides, arms swinging like pendulums. "Hi, Dad."

Beth stood in the doorway, saying a final good-bye to Matt. She closed the door, leaned against it, and stared viciously at her twin.

"Well, Ben, are you happy now?"

Ben stopped and looked at her curiously.

"Well? Are you?" she shouted. "You won't stop until you screw everything up!"

Ben took off for his room. Tillie jumped off my lap and hurried after him.

My recliner was upright now. "Okay, Beth," I said, "what happened?"

"If I tell you, you'll just take his side. You always rave when Ben does this, Ben does that!"

"I'm not sure about that. But if I do, maybe he doesn't get as many raves from other people as you do."

"Well, you spend more time with him."

"He *needs* more."

"C'mon, Dad. You know you care more about Ben!"

"That's baloney!"

"No it isn't!"

I took a breath and looked at the cheese in my hand, now squeezed into an unsightly ball. "What happened, honey?" I asked, keeping my voice down.

Beth burst into tears and the complaints poured out. Ben had shown up at basketball tryouts. During warmup, he had chased out onto the court and picked up loose balls the players could have retrieved themselves. Once when he scooted after a ball he had tripped a player going for a layup. Later, when Coach Rossi addressed the player and manager candidates sitting in the bleachers, Ben had sat next to Matt and "mimicked him." When Matt leaned back and put his elbows on the bench behind him, Ben did, too. And when Rossi was taking down the names of students trying out for manager and had ignored Ben's raised hand, Ben had yelled out, telling him to put down his name, too.

"Sounds like Ben did act a little strange," I said. "But Beth, nobody took time to help him act properly in that situation."

"See! There you go, defending him even before I'm done!"

35

"Sorry. Go on."

"Matt met me at the gym door, we started up Bannister Street, and guess who jumped out of a bush and walked home with us?"

"How many guesses do I get?"

Beth glared at me, seeing no humor in the situation.

"Aw c'mon, Beth, Matt understands. He grew up playing with your brother, and he's not had all that much to do with you since junior high."

"I know that. But we're in high school now and things can get rough."

"What?" I shouted. "What kind of kids go to Seahaven High? A bunch of prima donnas who go ape because a kid from special ed—just trying to be somebody, too—spooks them? I know what the problem is, Beth!"

"What?"

"You're afraid of losing Matt or you're ashamed of your brother! Which is it? Or is it both?"

Beth's face looked as if she'd been slapped. She folded her hands and stared at them, saying nothing for awhile. Then she looked up at me, her eyes narrowed and defiant. "I'll think about what you said, Dad. But can I tell you something you need to think about?"

"Sure."

"Okay, Dad. The world is not always going

to say 'please' or 'excuse me,' or 'good to have you here' to your precious son. And yet you keep encouraging him to bull his way into things . . ."

"Maybe, Beth. But I manage to be around when things get out of hand."

"That's right, Dad. But what will happen when you aren't around any longer?"

I stared at her with disbelief. I'd never heard her talk this way before.

Beth headed for her room, not waiting for an answer.

5 FOR ONCE MAGGIE was glad I'd forgotten the oven. When she came home I told her what had happened. She looked in on the kids and found both of them not hungry and wanting to stay in their rooms. Maggie and I made do with cereal and toast.

I pushed away my half-finished bowl and sat at the table, feeling I'd failed as a father. "I've been unfair, Mag. Beth's right."

"No, Andy. You touched her at a tender spot. She paid you back."

"But Maggie, I *have* given more time to Ben."

"Ben needs you more than she does, as you told her. I've never seen you turn your back on Beth when she needed you. Don't make such a big deal out of it, Andy. Remember those four big brothers of yours? Remember how they saw you as a noxious little brat they wanted out of their way?"

"I remember."

"And didn't they accuse your folks of loving you more than the rest?"

"All of us played that game, I guess."

"Well, why not Beth and Ben?"

I thought for a moment. "That makes sense.

But what about the other thing she said? *Do* I shove Ben in where he doesn't belong?"

"What's the matter with you, Banks? Are you going soft? He belongs *in the world*. After so many years of hiding the Bens-of-the-world away, it's going to take time for everyone to adjust. It'll take work, but it'll come."

"But will it come in time?" I questioned. "It shook me when Beth asked what would happen when I wasn't around."

"She knows that's a question we can't answer."

"Think I'll go talk to her."

"Don't, Andy. Ben needs you more now. I'll look in on Beth."

I reached over and framed Maggie's face with my palms, gave her a kiss, and headed for my son's room.

Ben was glued to his citizen's band receiver-transmitter, listening to Channel 19, the frequency used by travelers on I-95.

When he heard me, he leaned closer to the speaker and continued to listen while a trucker and an auto driver were cussing each other out. Anytime society slammed a door in Ben's face, he used his CB receiver to look in a window.

Saying nothing, I sat down on the bed. I knew my son would be too flustered for his tongue and lips to operate clearly right now. He was an excellent "receiver," but a poor "sender" in crises.

I glanced around the room. Above the bed was a Seahaven High banner, a newspaper photo of the school's football team, and a poster of Yankee outfielder Dave Winfield hitting a home run. Across the room was a stereo, with a stack of records too weird for my appreciation. Above the stereo there hung a poster of Bo Derek, wearing only a wet dress. Other things: a Boeing 747 model, binoculars, a football, a penknife, assorted pliers, screwdrivers, and hammers, Nike jogging shoes, four empty soda cans, and an aquarium that housed three paranoid hermit crabs. Anybody would swear an ordinary teenager lived here, I thought.

Then I thought about the way Ben's presence in our family had changed my world-view. It had been necessary to give up a number of attitudes, pursuits—even friends—because of Ben. I thought about the fresh viewpoints I had gained and the people who had filled the vacuum. Was I better for the losing and the gaining that had gone on in my life?

As I watched Ben trying to connect himself electronically to a world that didn't give him much, I sometimes wished I were a brilliant philosopher who could show others how much Ben could add to the world, if it let him.

6 TUESDAY, during supper, Ben worked hard at being proper in his sister's presence. No clowning, no hugs or shoulder rubs. Only carefully formed thank-yous when she passed the serving dishes. Beth also showed restraint, fearing that too much overt kindness would send him back to his CB radio.

Maggie and I watched out of the corners of our eyes while they both acted as if they'd recently returned from surgery and any sudden movement might tear stitches and open wounds. Their saccharine sweetness bothered me. It was a sign, nevertheless, that relations were on the mend.

After supper Ben excused himself and went back to his room. Beth held back momentarily to tell us, with some apprehension in her voice, that Ben had not shown up for basketball tryouts; that the coach had named Matt as team manager. Then Beth also disappeared behind her door for the rest of the evening.

A little later Ben's teacher, Polly Patterson, made a surprise visit.

"Ben sat in class like a Buddha today," she said. "No talk about composts or fat worms or heroes or wrestling or anything. He even

43

begged off taking notes to the principal so he could return with those glorious stories about what he saw 'regulars' doing. When our cocky Christopher Columbus is down, things get boring for all of us."

Maggie told Polly what had happened.

"Sounds like Beth and Ben are chasing after different stars," Polly said, "and colliding."

"Looks that way," Maggie agreed.

"What's with Beth and Matt now?" Polly asked.

"Still going together," Maggie told her. "But I don't know how close they are."

"And Ben?"

"He gave up on being manager," I said.

Polly gave me a searching look.

"Well, you know me, Polly," I said. "Maybe I have been trying to shape Ben into something he—"

"Shape Ben?" Polly exclaimed. "Are you kidding? Who are you, God?"

"He thinks he is around here," Maggie broke in, her lips tightening and curling into a smile.

"Look, Andy," Polly started again. "Ben has a specific talent—an incredible motivation. He has an uncanny ability to pick a single goal and go after it like few people I've ever seen."

"But, Polly, the kid could get flattened someday."

44

"I agree, Andy. And it's already happened a few times.

"But that's not the point. The point is this: You didn't make him that way. You may have given him some models—and you may have cheered him on. But you didn't give Ben his drive.

"Everyone tends to believe that all persons with Down's Syndrome function alike—that they all fit a single stereotype. Listen! There are kids with Down's Syndrome who have such severe handicapping conditions that they need someone to feed them and dress them—change their diapers, too. And some of those parents have as much moxie as you, Andy, even more. And there are other kids who are receiving regular graduation diplomas from high school —now that they're not being stereotyped and forced to function within the limits some latterday expert spelled out in a textbook.

"Look. Ben may always need a special education curriculum in some courses. But there are other subjects that regular teachers could teach him better than I can. I know that and so do you. Now if we can someday get regular teachers to know it, too . . ." She paused.

"In our class, Ben *is* our Christopher Columbus—always describing the uncharted lands some of my students will never experience first hand and . . ."

Polly stopped, and Maggie and I just sat there, not knowing how to respond.

"There I go again," Polly continued softly, "getting carried away." She chuckled under her breath. "Ben's a neat kid. I laugh when I recall the time he told the principal he had 'large nose holes'; or when he limped off the playground with a sprain and told the school nurse he had 'folded' his foot; or—best of all—when he comforted Sarah, telling her not to worry about her bird—he'd bring some of his best worms to feed it." Polly laughed. "All because he thought the visiting researcher said that Sarah might have a 'weak eagle' [ego]."

Polly stood up. "Well, hang in there, huh, guys?"

We nodded.

Polly walked toward the door, then stopped. "By the way, who is Mrs. Peck?"

I groaned.

"Mrs. Peck," Maggie said, "is our next-door neighbor on the east. You know how Ben gathers up our extra tomatoes from the garden and has a ball, going up and down the block giving them away?"

Polly nodded.

"Well, we saw Ben approach Beatrice Peck in her backyard. He held out a box of tomatoes, and she backed away so fast she tripped over the garden hose. Ben tried to help her up, but she wouldn't let him touch her."

"Was Ben hurt by that?"

"Don't know," Maggie answered. "He just told us he was sorry Mrs. Peck doesn't like tomatoes. Why? Does he mention her a lot at school?"

"Not often," Polly said. "Only about twice a day.

"I guess Ben and I are alike. I keep walking into the teacher's lounge, trying to convince the 'regulars' that their students should have more face-to-face interaction with my kids and help us get out of that off-to-the-side annex building. And Ben has his Mrs. Pecks."

Polly again started for the door and again stopped. She turned and grinned at us. "Can I tell you something about Matt O'Brien?"

"Sure," Maggie answered.

"He came out to the annex before school this morning. Said he was trying to learn about people with Down's Syndrome. I loaned him a book."

7 "HANDS OFF!"

We could hear scuffling in front of the TV.

"Darn you, Ben," Beth shouted, "I *have* to watch an hour special on the Civil War on PBS! It's for school."

"Ssschool?"

"Right!"

"Mmake a deal!"

"A deal?"

"Yep. Mmine afterward."

"The rest of the night?"

"Yep."

"You gotta be kidding. All night?"

"Yep."

"Aw gee, Ben! . . . Well, O.K."

"Deal! Shake!"

Maggie and I were in the kitchen doing the Wednesday evening dishes.

"Sounds like the twins are back to normal," she said, handing me a dish to wipe. "They've become a real pain in the neck to each other again."

"They're both going to be a pain in my neck if I want to watch any TV," I said. "But so what! We'll have a *normal* Thanksgiving tomorrow for a change."

"We've never minded waiting until after your bus run."

"Maybe not, but the chance to have an early dinner and a whole day at home makes me feel great."

The telephone rang. Ben scrambled for the extension in the front room. "Daaad. Sarah's father."

Mrs. Matlock's doctor had called Manny Rooney and said that since Sally and Maggie had been so helpful he'd appreciate it if some of the men in the parent group would meet with Mr. Matlock that evening in the Seahaven Hospital waiting room. Manny wanted Auggy Huff and me to meet him there in thirty minutes. I told him I would and hung up.

"The Matlocks are struggling right now," Maggie said.

"We can understand that."

As I went for my jacket the phone rang once more. Ben made another dash, gave his usual "Hello." Then he appeared in the kitchen, eyes wide and mouth forming a circle, trying to send out words that wouldn't come. Maggie took the receiver.

It was Aunt Phoebe. As soon as she learned that we were planning Thanksgiving at home, she gave Maggie an I'll-be-all-alone-in-New-York, followed by a relatives-ought-to-be-together-on-holidays-don't-you-think?

"You'd like to . . . to come here?" Maggie asked. "You . . . uh . . . 4:00? Well, Aunt Phoebe, we . . . well . . . All right. Goodbye."

By the time Maggie hung up, Ben and Beth were standing at her side, looking as if the Banks family had just received a death message.

"I can't believe it!" I said. "How could you let her do this to you?"

"She took me by surprise, Andy."

"I'll call her back."

"You can't."

"Why not?"

"She called from a pay phone in some restaurant."

I groaned. "Maggie, how could you—"

"Andy . . . I blew it! She came on so fast I—"

"Mag, you know I can't stand that woman. She's persuaded all your other relatives that she came up in the world after Uncle Frederick became a director of Metrobank, and she never stops reminding them that you would have been better off if you hadn't married me."

"She's wrong, Andy!"

"Maybe so, but she'll show up here and take control of everything."

"Her tongue has hands," Ben said.

I turned on him. "What the heck do you mean by that?"

"Sshe holds us with it."

"That's for sure! I remember watching Phoebe following Uncle Frederick's casket. It was the first time in her life she couldn't hold *him* with her tongue. Don't you see, Mag—"

"Stop it!" Maggie demanded. "You've made your point!"

I waited for her to say more, but she only glared at me.

"Aw . . . you guys," I said. "There I go, blowing up about something none of us are to blame for." I took a deep breath and looked at the three faces. "Sorry," I said. "I'll get with Manny and Auggy and cool down. Okay?"

The three faces nodded in unison.

***

"Barney," Manny called out, "more coffee over here when you have time."

"Comin' up," Barney answered.

"I can't get over it," Auggy said. "Mr. Matlock tellin' us we were the only pleasant faces he'd seen around his wife since their child was born."

"Interesting," Manny commented. "Hospital personnel are quick with 'cute' or 'beautiful' or 'healthy' or 'sweet' to most mothers."

"Yeah," Auggy agreed. "Then they turn to moms who have kids with disabilities, and their faces become sad and pitiful."

"I know," Manny said. "I've given hundreds of seminars to hospital workers on attitudes like that, but most of them still do it."

"At any rate," I said, "we got to Matlock just in time."

"Thanks for coming out with me, guys," Manny responded.

"Don't mention it," Auggy said. "You're the only 'perfessor' me'n Andy know how to talk to."

"I'll tell you a secret," Manny said. "I feel more at home with you than with some of my academic colleagues—like that psychologist who told Polly Patterson he thought Sarah might have a 'weak ego.' Besides . . . well, it's just that I have more in common with you guys."

Manny took a sip of coffee and started again. "And *now*, my *friends*, I need a couple of committee chairmen."

"Oh-oh," Auggy said. "Get too close to a 'perfessor' and you pay the price."

"Probably. I need a carpenter on a special committee—to build a positioning chair for one of the boys. Polly wants to get him out of his wheelchair more often, and with cerebral palsy, he needs support for his head. A manufactured one would cost $300 and still wouldn't be as good as a made-to-order one."

"I'll check in with Polly tomorrow," Auggy said.

"And what will my committee be doing?" I asked.

"Polly's students made some extra money collating and assembling some booklets. The class voted to buy tickets to the Christmas show in Rockefeller Center. She has the use of a school bus if she can find a driver."

"I'll take a vacation day at Greyhound," I said.

"Know what, Andy?" Auggie commented, pushing his cup away. "Have you noticed how often Manny assigns us to committees of one?"

"Yeah," I answered, getting up. "Have a good Thanksgiving, you guys."

Both wished me the same.

"Say, Andy," Manny added, "if you survive that aunt, come over and have a beer with Auggy and me after she leaves."

"Right!" seconded Auggy.

"Thanks. I'll need it."

8 IT WAS THANKSGIVING morning, and I alternated between whistling and humming as I emptied a pan of steaming giblets into a bowl of moist dressing that gave off the aroma of sage. Quickly checking on Maggie's whereabouts, I took a handful of meat. I was raising it to my mouth when a spatula flashed through the air and whacked me on the wrist.

"Okay, Big Shot," Maggie said, "cut it out!"

"Aw c'mon, Maggie. Just testing."

"Testing? You'll test 'til nothing's left. Now stir! We've got to get this turkey in the oven."

As I stirred, wind-driven torrents of rain splashed against the kitchen window. "Look at that," I said. "Weather man *said* warm air off the sea would smack into a cold front above us."

"He was right," Maggie agreed, "and we're in for more of the same all day."

"At any rate, it hasn't stopped the kids' activities."

At 8:00, Matt had appeared at our door, asking if Beth was up yet. She was—and she wasn't. She had dashed for the bathroom and Matt accepted an invitation to visit Ben at his listening post while he waited for her.

Since their fathers both earned their living on I-95, the boys felt at home with each other and swapped highway stories while the CB crackled in the background. Of course, most of the stories came from their dads. When I passed Ben's door, my son—his lips and tongue working hard—was describing one of my favorites; if he'd been reciting it for a test, he would have gotten an A+ for accurate recall.

Later, as Maggie held the turkey while I stuffed it, Beth, Matt, Ben, and Tillie sat in a circle on the living-room rug and talked. Every sentence seemed to end with laughter.

"Listen to those kids," Maggie said.

"I have been. They're something else this morning."

Maggie and I left the turkey and watched from the kitchen door.

"Show mme your hand," Ben said.

When Matt held out his right hand, Ben took it and pointed to the lines in the palm. "Ssee," he said, "you have an M."

"Uh-huh."

"Ssee mmine?"

Matt looked at the pudgy, straight-across crease that people like Ben have. "That's neat," Matt said.

"Think sso?" Ben said quickly. "Wanta trade?"

As we returned to our work, we heard Ben

explaining that some people with Down's
Syndrome have plastic surgery on their faces to
make them look more like other people.

"That's great," Matt said.

"*Grreat?*" Ben said. "How'd ya *know* me
then?"

More laughter.

"Sounds like Ben's getting carried away," I
said, "and Beth's letting it happen."

"She'll handle it," Maggie said.

Ben began putting hammerlocks, full nelsons, and half nelsons on a willing Matt.

Feeling nervous about Ben being the whole
show, I peeked in again, just in time to see him
putting a takedown on Matt and chaining it into
a pin-hold.

"Way ta go," Matt said from the bottom.
"You know your stuff."

"Yep," Ben said. "Like wressstling. Nnnot
boxing."

"Why not?"

"People ssshouldn't bang each other's
brains."

Beth continued to sit back and do nothing.

"Maybe I better slow Ben down."

"Stay here!" Maggie said. "Beth will handle
it."

Ben began his rundown on good gardening
and the need for "ssuper-fat worms." Of
course, this explanation could never be com-

plete without a show-and-tell. Ben rose to his feet, prepared to fetch samples of his wrigglers.

"No, Ben!" Beth let out a screech that shook the house and stopped her brother cold.

"Beth handled it," Maggie said, looking up with a wry smile.

Someone knocked at the back door.

Maggie stretched to peer out the kitchen window. "It's Joanne and Rich."

"Come in," I shouted. "Door's open."

"Can we have our son back?" Joanne asked. "We have to be on our way to Boston."

"Rough weather, Big Rich," I said.

"Yeah. Rather be doing it in my eighteen-wheeler. That car makes me feel like I'm strapped into a roller skate."

"Know what you mean," I said. "Give our best to your sister and her family."

"Sure will, Andy. Too bad you don't have any relatives to get with."

"We do."

"You do?" Joanne wondered. "You don't have any relatives around . . . Oh no! The aunt in New York."

"You got it," Maggie said.

Joanne looked at Maggie, making sure she heard right. Then she rolled her eyes and looked at us sadly.

"Look," Big Rich said, "I hope the whole day won't be lost—I mean . . . we'll see ya when we get back." He turned toward the living room. "C'mon, Matt. Time to go."

As soon as they were gone, Beth came to me, her eyes sparkling. She placed her head against my chest. I put my arms around her and hugged her.

Then the telephone rang. It was Phoebe, calling to say she wasn't about to drive to Seahaven in *this* storm. Besides, she and "my very dear friend, Regina Ruth Kensington"— whoever that was—had managed to get reservations for Thanksgiving dinner at Skyview Gardens on the top floor of the Epicenter Building, and "surely you must understand that this is a once-in-a-lifetime opportunity, and after all, relatives like us are always available in time of . . ."

I stopped listening and began a smile that spread to the others who could hear the shrill voice overflowing the receiver. Ben pointed his toes inward, put his knees together and bent over with his hand on his mouth, frantically trying to keep from snickering out loud.

"We understand, Phoebe . . . Of course, Phoebe . . . Goodbye, Phoebe."

"Well, folks," I said, hanging up the phone, "the woman with the hands on her tongue has let go!"

"Okaaay!" Ben shouted.

Maggie adjusted the oven control, raising it

by 50°. "Beth, remind me to baste more often."

Beth nodded as she put on an apron.

"Ben," Maggie said, "set the table."

Ben scrambled for the drawer containing the silverware.

"Andy, I want you to put the mincemeat in the pie shells. On second thought, Beth, you do the pies. Andy, peel the potatoes."

When everyone had finished the assigned tasks, we stood around the kitchen awaiting a prediction.

"We can expect dinner in an hour and a half," Maggie announced.

"Go for it!" Ben shouted.

"Tell you what," Maggie said. "Beth, get your guitar and teach us that song you wrote."

"Aw, Mom," Beth said, "it's not that big a deal."

"After winning first place in lyric competition, advanced-music class no less? Come on!"

Beth sat cross-legged on the living-room rug and tuned her guitar. "Look, it's not that—"

"Quit being modest," Maggie ordered. "Sing."

Beth looked at the strings, stroked the opening chords and filled the room with her soft contralto.

What is life about
How can I find out?

Can I really know?
Does anybody know?

What is life about?
How can I find out?
If I find no clue,
Here's what I will do.

I will reach outside myself,
And work at helping you.
I will look beyond myself,
And try to love you, too.

To love and work with you.
I'll try to do these two.
That's what I will do.
That's what I will do.

As Beth's voice trailed away, I couldn't find
words to tell her how the song had touched me.
Of course, I'd heard her in her room, playing
certain parts over and over again. But hearing it
now left me breathless. Was I overreacting
because of all the trouble this past week? Then I
noticed a tear on Maggie's cheek, and I knew
the kid was good. Right then I resolved to
praise Beth's achievements, encourage her as
much as I did Ben.
"Beth," I said, "that was . . . beautiful."
Beth looked straight at me, her eyes shining.

"How'd you make up the words?" I asked.

"From watching the way my brother keeps charging into the world and trying to figure it out. I've watched Ben striding through the hall at Seahaven High with notes for the principal. I've watched him hundreds of times when he didn't know it. There Ben would go, his arms swinging and his head looking around as if it were a radar antenna—trying to collect every sight and sound and make sense of them."

Beth ducked her head and ran her fingers nervously over the strings. "But then I'd get so mad at him for butting into my business I'd never tell any of you."

I pondered what Beth had said. Then I spoke softly. "Sounds like all of us have changed a bit this week."

"Yep." Ben's voice was as soft as mine. Then he straightened his back, held his head high, and turned on his grin. "Teach us," he said.

The four of us went over the lyrics again and again. Even though Ben has some tone deafness, he sings loudly and with gusto. His frequent flats didn't diminish our spirits, or his.

When all the wonderful smelling food was on the table and we sat down, everyone waited for Maggie's starting signal.

"I know we won't ever win a prize for being religious," Maggie said, "but maybe we ought to say something resembling a Thanksgiving prayer. Who'll volunteer?"

"You, Dad," Ben spoke up.

"Right," Beth agreed. "It's time you cleaned up your language anyway."

My look of pained innocence drew jeers and snickers until I bowed my head and started to speak. "Well, here we are. The Banks family. And we are reaching outside ourselves. If you hear us, we admit that we don't know much about you or what you have in mind for us. That's okay. We don't have to know everything. But if you had anything to do with putting us together, we'd like to say *thanks*. We couldn't have made a better arrangement if we had done it ourselves."

I carved the turkey and the feast began. The food was rich and the laughter loud. When I could eat no more, I gave a satisfied sigh, got up, and headed for the living room and the TV.

"Oh no you don't!" Maggie said. "No football today!"

I stopped and grabbed my side as if I'd been shot.

"To the kitchen, clown," Maggie continued. "Remember the dirty dishes? What shall we do with them?"

"Dishes? I'll tell you what we shall do with the dishes, Mrs. Banks. We shall leave them! We shall jump into our little yellow Pinto, drive down I-95, and go to the cut-rate 'twi-night' movie in Havenville."

"All right, Mr. Banks," Maggie said, taking off her apron and flinging it like a flamenco dancer, "get your engine warmed up!"

***

A sheet of rain covered the windshield, and I slowed down until the wipers could do their stuff.

"Be careful, Andy," Maggie said from the back seat.

"I'll stay in the right lane and let the crazies slosh by."

Ben turned to the women in the back. "You're safe. Dad's the best. Let's sing mmy song."

"*Your* song?" Beth sounded astonished.

"That's what you said."

Beth led off and the rest of us joined in, singing "Ben's Song." Our singing is the last thing I remember as we slowed down for the tollgate.

9   WE WERE SINGING—and then
we weren't. That's strange, I said to myself.
What happened? Why can't I see the windshield wipers swishing back and forth? What
happened to all the lights? Why aren't we
singing "Ben's Song" anymore?

I was floating in darkness—dense and
enveloping darkness—broken, suddenly, by a
tiny circle of light high above. The blackness
slowly lessened and I caught sight of blurred
forms moving, nodding, speaking. Whoever
they were, they spoke softly, but one question
came through as if by a public-address system:
"Mr. Banks, can you hear me?"

I tried to make out the shapes. The strain of
focusing made me breathe faster and I came
close to slipping back into blackness. But I kept
trying. I had to know why I was "in here," why
everybody else was "out there," and why my
family and I weren't singing anymore.

"Mr. Banks, can you hear me?" the voice
repeated.

I tried to move my jaws. Nothing happened.

"Mr. Banks, if you can't speak, don't try."

I relaxed. My focus improved until I could see
an athletic looking man, probably in his

early thirties, with coal-black curly hair and a well-trimmed beard. His dark eyes watched me as if I were one of the most valuable persons in his life.

"Mr. Banks, if you can hear me, close your eyes—once."

I took two deep breaths. Then I carefully closed my eyes, opened them wide and waited.

"Mr. Banks, I'm Dr. Slocum. You're in Seahaven Hospital. You've been in an accident. You were slowing down for the Midhaven Tolls. The driver behind you said he was blinded by a heavy sheet of rain and . . . well, he hit you."

Dr. Slocum paused and studied my eyes. "Can you see me?" he asked.

I closed and opened my eyes.

"Good. You have some bad burns on the face and . . . " He stopped.

I kept looking at him until he started to speak again. "You have a linear fracture on the right side of the head, some internal injuries, especially some serious bleeding around a kidney, and . . ."

He stopped again. He could tell from my eyes that I wasn't interested in all that clinical jargon.

"Mr. Banks, your son is okay. He was thrown clear and received only minor scratches and bruises. He's staying with your neighbors, the O'Briens."

Slocum looked away. Although I couldn't move my head, my eyes followed him. When he sensed that I was watching his every move, every expression, he turned and stared at the thick, almost horizontal limb of a giant oak tree just outside the window.

I watched the back of his head.

He slowly turned to face me. "Mr. Banks," he said and picked up my left hand, holding it with both of his. "I . . . Mr. Banks, your wife and daughter couldn't get out."

I searched Dr. Slocum's face. They couldn't get out? What did he mean by that? Then I remembered a thud and a whirling and a grating and our yellow Pinto in flames and screams and sirens and trying to reach out to the rest of the family—and my heart ripping apart when I couldn't.

I searched the doctor's face again for some inkling that it was all a bad dream—that it didn't really happen. I found none. I looked to him for help. And when I saw there was nothing he could do, I shivered. Then I felt myself floating downward away from the circle of light until it vanished.

10 WHEN I REGAINED conscious-
ness, my whole being throbbed. I felt as if a
giant hand had swept out of nowhere and
struck me with such force it had loosened every
bone in my body. I was flat on my back, unable
to move; my limbs felt as if they were attached
with rubber bands. A room full of people
surrounded me, checked my various parts, and
whispered their findings.

When many hands held me and wrapped my
head, I thought I'd go out of my mind with
pain. Then came the vomiting, and I wondered
whether I'd shake myself to pieces before they
could bind me up. I welcomed the bandaging of
my head, leaving openings for only my nose
and mouth. That helped me hide away, like
Ben's hermit crabs, from the world-gone-
vicious around me.

Then I discovered that the agony inside my
head was worse. The idea of never seeing
Maggie and Beth again ripped me up so badly
that I tried to shove it out of my mind. I forced
myself to think about the many times Ben and I
had stopped our gardening on a lazy summer
afternoon, picked up the frisbee we kept on the
lawn, and sailed it to each other. We had kept it

up for hours on end. Saying nothing. Just floating it back and forth. Then I wondered if I'd ever spin a frisbee to Ben again. Or would somebody else take my place?

Next, thoughts welled up about Tillie. Who would let her out in the morning and feed her and change her water?

Who would the dispatcher get to take over my bus run? Who would speak out for Ben at the special-ed parent meetings, who would meet him at Barney's and go with him to the statue?

Then when I really felt powerless and useless and smashed down, the memories of Maggie and Beth pushed their way in. I thought about how I used to tease them and pinch their cheeks until they laughed and about how we wrapped our arms around each other. But the giant hand, with a single blow, had made an impossible canyon between them and me. How could I go on living, knowing I'd never hug them again?

"The patient's blood pressure has gone up," someone said.

"His breathing is uneven and increasing," someone else said.

I started sliding into unconsciousness again. Thank God, I thought. Now the agony will stop.

It didn't. Dr. Slocum showed up in a dream,

staring at me, looking worried. Then he lifted a giant shovel high and slammed it down, cutting me in half, leaving me writhing like Ben's earthworms when a spade sliced them accidentally.

A few moments later, Maggie and Beth appeared. They didn't speak, but they looked as if they wanted me to do something. I tried to reach out and hold them. Then they vanished.

"He may be in pain, Doctor," I heard someone say. "Shouldn't we give him a sedative?"

There was a long silence. I tried to scream through my teeth that I did need something. When I couldn't, I waited for him to answer.

"I wish I could," Slocum spoke softly. "But I can't risk pain killers until I get a diagnosis on his head injuries."

When I heard that, it suddenly seemed that all the physical and emotional pain in the world must be trapped within my being. My muscles tightened like violin strings and my whole body began to shake. Then, as if the giant hand had snapped its fingers, the pain stopped. I seemed to be floating in fluid. Death is on its way, I thought, and I wanted it to come. Then I felt nothing.

11   "WHADAYAMEAN, you dread seein' Christmas come? You should complain! How'd ya like to be that guy in 205? He loses a wife and a daughter; and if he lives, all he has left to go home to is a retard. Now if . . ."

A passing jet drowned the sounds of the man and his mop bucket in the hall. When the jet was gone, I was gone, too, at least for a day.

***

" . . . is the anniversary of the Day of Infamy. On December 7, in 1941, Japanese dive bombers swooped down on Battleship Row. Two hours later, 18 ships were sunk or heavily damaged, more than 188 aircraft were destroyed and 2,403 American lives were lost.

"In other news, the President, at a 4:00 press conference, will reveal . . ."

I was gone again before the voice from a radio in another room said what the President planned to reveal. It didn't matter.

***

" . . . been unconscious ten days. I'm baffled." It was Dr. Slocum whispering.

"What about the brain injury, Tom?" another man said.

"Can't really tell. There may be some complications. Part could be due to a stroke. Or it could be one of those paralyzing stress reactions like the GIs experienced in battle. Losing a wife *and* a daughter is one heavy psychological blow."

"And the kidney you mentioned?"

"Lots of swelling and blood. If it breaks loose . . ."

***

"Mrs. O'Brien called," a nurse said outside my door. "Said Ben was gone again and if he shows up here, to call."

"He'll show up all right," another nurse said.

"Well, when he does, that kid Matt will come get him. Mrs. O'Brien said not to make any big deal out of it."

Hearing my son's name set off a twinge of feeling for a moment . . . then it faded.

***

The door opened and I heard someone walking quietly to my side. I could tell that two hands began to rub my shoulders, even though I couldn't actually feel them.

The door opened again and someone else

stood beside my bed, saying nothing while the hands continued their work.

Then the hands stopped.

"C'mon, Ben," Matt said. "You've done all you can. Let's go home."

***

" . . . eleven more days until Christmas, and Sholer's Department Store remains open until 10:00 each evening for your shopping convenience. And now, for your listening pleasure . . ."

***

"That Banks kid is here again. I sat him down at the nurses' station with some paper and crayons and told him to draw some pictures until the O'Briens came. Do you know what he kept drawing? Cars with smoke coming out of them."

***

"How I hate this cold! What I wouldn't give to be in Florida for Christmas and . . ."

***

" . . . call the O'Briens. Tell them 205's son is on that tree limb outside the window again."

***

" . . . and let's leave the eyes clear as we rebandage the head this time."

I kept my eyes closed tightly until everyone had left. When I opened them, I could see. But in my fuzzy state, sights, like sounds, didn't seem to penetrate my mind.

***

With eyes barely cracked, I noticed the door opening slowly. Ben appeared. He moved toward me holding one of my old cigar boxes with a red ribbon tied around it. He approached my bed like a shepherd approaching the Christmas manger. He put the box down, raised his hand and, with palm open, made a circular motion.

"Ben! You can't come in here," a nurse said. "If I've told you once, I've told you—Oh! That's nice. You've brought your father a present. Let's see if it's something we can leave in the—Oh, good grief! Get those worms out of here!"

***

"Did ya hear on the morning news how some guy got a bravery award from some New York organization for pulling 205 away from that burning car?"

"Yeah. And the guy kept saying 205's son was right there, pulling with him."

"Makes ya wonder why they didn't give the kid an award."

"Guess they thought you have to have brains to be a hero."

***

". . . rain and sleet turning to snow on this morning of December 21. By the way, folks, today is the shortest day of the year. The storm warning extends . . ."

***

" . . . been hanging on the edge for days. He doesn't seem to feel anything, no urge to live—nothing."

"You've done everything you could, Tom. Just ease up. Sometimes you get overly involved with your patients and when you do . . ."

***

"There's been a steady string of 205's friends at the desk asking about him this afternoon—the O'Briens, that school teacher, the guy who runs the diner on the square. Even that carpenter and his wife showed up with the two professors from the college."

"Has anything happened to 205?"

"Nope. But something must be happening out there."

77

Although I could still hear the words, they sounded strange and far away. It was as if I were swimming underwater.

Then I began to float away again, down toward darkness. Light or darkness—it made no difference to me.

***

"Oh no! Look at that blood pressure!" a distant, muffled voice shouted.

"Call the code!"

I heard a starched dress crackling and rubber-soled shoes running from the room.

Was this it? Must be, I thought. I felt weightless. More and more darkness came over me, calming me, soothing me like the comforter my mother used to tuck around me as a child. I'm going, I thought. No stopping me now.

And yet my ears hadn't quit. I heard speakers in the hall blaring: Code 99—Second Floor—and I knew it was for me. I sensed the room filling with people who grabbed for my pulse and sent fluids into me through needles and tubes.

Dr. Slocum rushed in. "Get him to surgery on the double!"

Arms lifted me onto a cart, wheeled me out of the room. "Now wait a minute, Tom," someone said, running alongside the cart. "Don't you think—"

"Look, Doctor, Banks is my patient!"

"Take it easy, Tom. I know. But have you forgotten what you said this morning?"

"Never mind! I'm thinking of that son of his."

"Ease up, Tom."

"I want to," Slocum said. "But I've caught Ben in the halls, I've chased him out of the room. I've even pulled him down from that tree. How can I face Ben if his dad dies?"

"He'll be okay, Tom. You told me temporary guardianship papers were being signed. Those O'Briens—they'll take good care—"

"It wasn't the O'Briens. Some relative, Phoebe Preston, Paxton—something like that . . ."

12   DR. SLOCUM leaned over me, looked into my eyes. "Mr. Banks, you had emergency surgery yesterday. Some bleeding broke loose around your kidney. We stopped it. Now I need to know how *you* feel you're doing." He paused. "If you feel you're doing okay, close your eyes once. Not okay, close them twice."

I signaled once, even though the incision on the right side of my navel was sore and I felt so weak it would have been impossible to move a finger even if I could have.

"You know, Mr. Banks, I had decided to cancel surgery—but then you opened your eyes—not much, but enough to show you were doing your darndest . . ."

I closed my eyes once to let him know he was right.

"But you went pale on us, your blood pressure went to sixty over forty, and I knew the hematoma had . . ."

Slocum stopped. He must have seen the anger in my eyes. I didn't want to know about that! I wanted to know what Phoebe was up to! I wanted Slocum to get the truth about Phoebe from the O'Briens.

"Your breathing's getting heavy," Slocum said. "Do your best to relax. Your vital signs . . . I mean—your condition is better than before." Slocum patted me on the arm and left.

I set my mind to staying as calm as possible, but I also pledged myself to *stay conscious* as long as I could. Build your endurance, I said to myself. Stop trying to hide in darkness, no matter how much thoughts of the death of Maggie and Beth tear at you. Don't pity yourself; shake it off and *stay conscious*. Keep those eyes open—open wide.

I told myself to focus on the ceiling. *Look!* There are 14 squares of celotex touching the side wall and 10 squares across. I know Maggie's dead—*count*. Multiply 14 times 10; makes 140 full squares. There's a gouge in the fourth square up, second one over. *Study!* How did it get there? There are six other strange marks—*focus*. Stay with the first and leave the other six for later.

I began to feel dizzy. I closed my eyes and rested until it stopped. Then back to those marks above me. Today, the ceiling. Tomorrow, the right wall.

The door opened and a nurse entered with a hypodermic needle on a small tray. "Dr. Slocum ordered this for you," she said. "It'll keep you under for awhile."

I stared at the needle as if it were an executioner's dagger and then I stared at the nurse, trying to tell her, No!

But she was looking at my arm. She took it in one hand and the needle in the other. Then she put the needle down, took my arm in both hands and began to massage it. "My goodness!" she exclaimed. "Your muscles are like rocks." She stopped for a moment and studied the arm. Then she quickly took the needle and stuck it in.

13

". . . AND NOW A WORD from our sponsor. Sholer's Department Store wants to remind all you late shoppers that today is Thurday, December 23. If you feel frustrated and helpless when choosing Christmas gifts, come into Sholer's on the square. Let our experienced salespeople . . ."

A door closed somewhere, muffling the sound. Other voices and the clanking of steel utensils more than filled the void. I wondered why the streets around this place were lined with signs that read Hospital—Quiet Zone.

Then I saw the first beams of the rising sun. I watched it out of the corner of my eye as it loomed larger and larger, a morning haze magnifying it into a giant cherry-red ball. What a view! As it rose, it became smaller and brighter until a comforting warmth penetrated my cheek. I could feel the sun. I could *feel* the *sun!*

Imagine that! I said to myself. I've greeted more sunrises than any man I know, outside of Big Rich, but none ever felt as good as this one. I prayed for more—lots more.

Dr. Slocum came in and checked me with his

stethoscope. "Things sound good, Mr. Banks. Do you feel like seeing Ben?"

I signaled quickly.

"Thought so," he said. "He'll be in after school. He can only stay for a few minutes. You're still wiped out; got to get more rest."

Slocum studied the limb outside my window. "Someday," he said, "I hope I'll have a son as crazy about me as Ben is about you."

When Slocum left, I felt as I had on a Friday many years ago, when I called Maggie and asked for our first date—halfway expecting her to turn me down. When she didn't, I took two baths and shaved three times. Ben's forthcoming visit set my heart beating and my blood flowing the same way.

An hour later, Barney Kowalski stepped in for a minute. He wasn't sure what it was okay to talk about. So he waved hello, looked kindly at me, said four times that he missed me at the diner, gave me some pats on the arm, and waved goodbye.

Joanne stopped in to say that Polly was bringing Ben as soon as school was out, that Big Rich was on his way back from a run to Montreal; he'd see me tomorrow. Then she looked me straight in the eye and said, "Andy, you have just got to get well!" She leaned over, kissed me on the cheek, and left quickly, to keep from crying, I suspected.

Heather Pendleton, Beth's school chum, who had ditched a study hall, got permission from a nurse to come in for a second. "Had to let you know I care about you," she said, "and . . . well, Mr. Banks, if you need another kid around, let it be me." She waited momentarily for an answer I could not speak. Then she blew me a kiss and left.

Manny and Sally took their lunch hour from the college to collect Georgia Huff from home and Auggy from a construction site.

"Came to say we're pulling for you," Auggy said.

The others backed him up with "Right" and "Yeah" and "That's for sure."

"We want you back with us soon," Sally said.

More murmurs of agreement from the others.

I closed my eyes and opened them, trying to let them know I understood. But they didn't know the code. So I just looked as lovingly as I could at those friends who had so much in common with me.

I could tell they had other things they wanted to say. But how could they discuss them with a man who was barely alive and unable to respond?

Then came more pats and kisses and We'll-be-back-soons and Hang-in-theres and Bye-Andys.

I knew why they had all come in one after the other. Phoebe had to be up to something, and I was the only one who could stop her. Even so, I shoved the problem to the back of my mind.

Ben and Polly would walk through the door soon, and I could hardly wait to see them.

At 3:10, the door opened. Ben stood there for a moment, then walked slowly and stiffly to the bed. He didn't wave or say Hi or hug me. I could tell something was wrong, and I waited for Polly to appear. Phoebe Paxton appeared instead.

Her feet clicked off short, rapid steps to bring her tiny sinewy body around the foot of the bed. Then her 65-year-old-but-trying-to-look-20 face under the impeccable permanent in the red-dyed hair appeared next to Ben's and a couple of feet above mine.

"Hello, Andrew," she said. "How are you feeling?"

She waited.

"I'm sorry, Andrew, I keep forgetting you can't talk."

She waited again, then began twisting a ring on her finger. Ben remained rigid.

"Well, Andrew, the doctor said you can understand me, so I'll tell you what's happened. My attorney, Reginald Battersby, after many discussions with our relatives in Nebraska, had a conference with Dr. Slocum. The doctor signed papers saying you're unable to manage your affairs. Since I'm the only blood relative nearby, I felt obliged to take power of attorney . . . and to become Ben's guardian."

I stared at her. Then I began to breathe deeply.

"Please understand, Andrew. I *had* to do it. Your neighbor Beatrice Peck said so, too. I met her at the funeral, and I asked her to make regular collect calls to tell me how things were going. Then it became clear to both of us that this poor child, who is suffering from a mental condition—and now a tragedy—is acting so . . . well, so strange that he needs professional help, people who *understand* his condition."

She stopped again and looked at me as if I'd surely break silence. She watched and waited, then spoke slowly, making sure every word came out clearly.

"Andrew, I have arranged for Ben to be sent to the Haven for the Handicapped on Long Island. It is a highly respected residence for twenty retarded males, according to the executive director. He said Ben would have his own room, a daily schedule of activities and . . . Andrew, he'll be with his own kind."

Phoebe evaded eye contact and kept talking. "The O'Briens—bless their hearts—tried to manage Ben, and they even said they would not give him up. But Beatrice told me to use my lawyer and stick by my guns.

"So . . . Andrew . . . the director is in the waiting room and . . . I'll keep you informed. Come, Ben."

Ben moved away slowly, with Phoebe behind him. His eyes, pleading for me to do something—*anything*—watched me until he disappeared through the door.

By then the room was moving and that old numbness began to creep over me again. Quickly I began to count the ceiling tiles.

14   ". . . AND EVEN though it's the day before Christmas, Sholer's Department Store wants to remind you they'll remain open tonight until 7:00. And now for the news. A White House spokesman . . ."

Somebody had opened the door of the room where the radio was blaring the early morning news, and I wondered how many other patients were fed up with such a rude awakening. Next I felt the sun blinding me. If the nurses really cared, I thought, they'd close the curtains.

Slocum arrived. "How are you?"

I looked away.

"Mr. Banks?"

I continued to look away.

Slocum turned to the window for a moment. Then he left.

Thirty minutes later he returned with Polly Patterson.

"Mr. Banks," he said, "I called Miss Patterson. We talked. And I think you may be angry because I signed the attorney's . . ."

I blinked quickly and glared at him.

"Mr. Banks, Mrs. Paxton is a relative and I thought . . ."

I looked away again and he stopped.

"Andy," Polly said, "Dr. Slocum didn't know."

"Miss Patterson explained the situation," Slocum said, "and all this can be solved if we can get you well. You're looking better, but that kidney surgery leaves a person drained. Once you get your strength back—and that'll take time—then . . . But there's something else you need to know." Slocum nodded to Polly.

"Andy," she began, "Ben ran off. As soon as he got outside with the man from Long Island, he took off as fast as he could go.

"All of us who know Ben covered the town, looking for him last night. We didn't find him, but we know he entered your house sometime after midnight. Someone saw him leaving on the run at daybreak."

"Your friends are back on the streets this morning," Slocum said. "When they find your son, I plan to join them for a serious talk with Mrs. Paxton."

"Andy," Polly said, "I know Ben's okay. He's tough."

"In the meantime," Slocum said, "I'm putting a No Visitors sign on your door. You've got to get your strength back."

After they left, I lay perfectly still, trying to think health back into my body.

That evening, I counted all kinds of things in

the room. My ears, nevertheless, were tuned for news from the outside.

***

"Wow! Never saw the place so quiet."
"Yeah. Only folks here are those who have to be."

***

"Did you see the snow coming down? It's going to be a white Christmas for sure."

***

" . . . although it is 7:00 P.M. Eastern Standard Time, it is midnight in Bethlehem where pilgrims have gathered in the Church of the Nativity, the oldest Christian church in use, for the annual candlelight service . . . "

***

"Bring the buckets over here. Soon as we get this floor done, boss says we can go home early."
"Aaall right!"

***

The stores on the square closed for the holiday, and the snow continued to fall, and it became colder, and nobody came with news of Ben.

After the cleaning crew put away their equipment and left, only distant echoing sounds came from the hall. Surely someone will be coming in, I thought. Then I heard a man's leather-soled oxfords striking the floor at a distance, coming closer until my door opened.

It was a tired looking Dr. Slocum. "Mr. Banks, I have to tell you, we haven't found Ben yet." He paused. "But you can't do anything about it. You must trust your friends." Then I saw the syringe in his hand. "This will let you sleep soundly until tomorrow morning."

I didn't hear another thing until that radio woke me up.

" . . . another tragic turn of events for a Seahaven family last night . . . "

"Hey! Open that door," someone said, "I want to hear the rest of that."

". . . Officer Harry Brill reported finding Benjamin Banks, the 16-year-old mentally retarded son of Andrew and the late Margaret Banks, huddled in the burned-out back seat of the family automobile now at Carruthers Used Auto Parts. According to Brill, the Banks youth was violent and bit the officer on the arm when he tried to restrain him.

"The youth was taken to the High Ridge Developmental Center for an emergency admission.

"On Thanksgiving Day, the Banks—"

"Close that door!" Dr. Slocum shouted. "Don't you people have any sense at all? Are you trying to kill my patient?"

Slocum entered, took a look at me and left. He returned with a nurse and another syringe.

15   ON SUNDAY MORNING, the day after Christmas, there was no sun. The aftereffects of Slocum's sedations had left me groggy and depressed. My stomach churned and hardened and threatened to make me vomit.

I was more aware than ever of my precarious condition. One more blow from the outside or something else breaking loose on the inside, and I'd be finished.

And yet, Phoebe and her lawyer were waiting in the wings to dispose of Ben in a way they claimed would be more humane than the way I had raised him. I knew that if I died now, my last conscious thought would be filled with agony.

Slocum walked into the room and, like a machine, listened through his stethoscope to my heart and lungs, forced my eyes open and shone a light into them. Then as he felt and poked various areas of my body, without even glancing at my face, he spoke in a monotone. "A Mr. Laveck, Ben's social worker at High Ridge, telephoned. Said he wanted to come in this morning and talk to me. I called Miss Patterson and she said she and some of your friends would meet with him, too. Do you want him to drop in and see you for a moment?"

"Yy."

Slocum straightened up and looked at my face.

"Say that again."

"Yyyy."

He reached over and touched the right side of my mouth. "Once more."

"Yyyyyeeh!"

Slocum walked quickly to the foot of the bed, pulled the covers back, and held my left foot. "Try to wiggle your toes."

They moved.

He came to my side and took my left hand. My fingers moved.

"Mr. Banks," he said softly, "good going."

***

At 2:00, Slocum returned with a tall, slender, slightly graying man in his late forties. The lines at the corners of his eyes and the way he moved gave him the appearance of a thoughtful, sensitive person.

"This is Fred Laveck," Slocum said.

"Hello, Mr. Banks."

"Mr. Banks can hear," Slocum said, "but he still has trouble responding."

"I understand. After meeting with your

friends, Mr. Banks, I feel I know you well. I'll do everything I can to look out for your son's interests. High Ridge is only thirty-five miles away and—"

"Tl."

Both men looked closely at my lips.

"Try again," Slocum said.

"Tlll."

"Till? Are you trying to say a word?"

I blinked.

"Okay. Try again."

"Tlllll."

"Hm," Slocum said, watching my eyes. "Toll? The tollgate? Tale? Tell?"

I blinked.

"Got it! It's *tell*."

"Buh. Tllbuh."

I tried better than a dozen times, until Slocum was actually perspiring. "Let's stop now," he said. "Rest. We'll work on it some more later." He and Laveck headed for the door.

"Tlll Buh en!" I struggled to make them understand.

Slocum suddenly stopped in his tracks, whirled, and hit the side of his head with his palm. "Of course. *Tell Ben*! You want to see Ben!"

"Yyyy."

Slocum hesitated and looked to Laveck for an answer.

"I'll talk to the other staff members," Laveck said.

***

At 7:00, Laveck and Slocum entered the room with Ben.

As soon as I saw him, I wanted to hold my arms out to him, but I could barely raise my right one before it felt like rubber and dropped to my side. And Ben walked up to the bed as waxy as when he had been with Phoebe.

Ben stood two steps away from the bed.

"Ben, you can say hello to your dad," Laveck said.

"H'lo."

"You can pat him on the arm if you like," Laveck said.

Ben's hand rose mechanically, gave me a pat. Then he returned to Laveck's side.

I tried to make a sound, but I was so upset from seeing how sad he looked that nothing worked. All I could do was watch while he stood there like someone readying himself for a death sentence.

"Ben," Laveck said, "your father can't speak to you, but I know he's glad to see you."

Ben looked up at Laveck.

"He asked to see you," the social worker said.

"Not mmmad at me?"

100

"What do you mean, Ben?" Laveck said.

Ben slowly turned his head toward me, his brow furrowed. "Don't be mmmmmad, Dad. Tried! . . . People grabbed mmme. . . . Held me!"

Tears flooded his eyes.

"Tell mmme . . . not mmmad!" Ben began to sob as the two men led him out of the room.

A few minutes later, Slocum and Laveck came back.

"Mr. and Mrs. O'Brien and Matt met us in the hall," the doctor said. "Ben's with them in the waiting room. Mr. Laveck wanted to speak to you for a moment."

"Mr. Banks," Laveck said, "what happened here a few minutes ago helped me to understand what has been going on with Ben. Ever since his admission to High Ridge, he has been too quiet, sitting on his bed or in a corner in the day room, not speaking, not defending himself when other boys picked on him."

Laveck leaned against the wall and took a deep breath. "Now this is a quick opinion: Some people admitted to the institution harbor secret feelings that they're there because they've committed some terrible wrong. Staff members keep telling them they are there because they need help. But it doesn't sink in."

"And now we know what Ben thinks he's done," Slocum said.

"It appears that way."

"And now we can tell him he's not to blame."

"It's not that easy."

"Mr. Laveck, do you feel Ben belongs at High Ridge?"

"No sir."

"Why not?"

"No institution can even begin to replace his family."

"And the O'Briens?"

"We couldn't come close to them either."

"Then let's get him back there."

"We can't. Legally, Mrs. Paxton speaks for Mr. Banks if he can't speak for himself. I've had repeated talks with her, and I assure you, she insists that Ben should stay with us. In time, tests and professional judgments could over-rule her."

"Then I'll revoke my signed statement," Slocum declared.

"If you do, she'll show up with outside evaluators and force a competency hearing with doctors, lawyers, a judge—the whole works. Are you ready for that now?"

Slocum hesitated. "So Ben has to go back with you?"

"I'm afraid so."

Slocum stared at the floor.

"Tllbuh."

Slocum looked up. "Tell Ben?"

"Yyy. Nn mmmm."

"The O'Briens may be able to help," Slocum said, and went to bring Big Rich and Matt in.

"He's trying to say something. He wants us to tell Ben something."

All faces looked at me again. I tried to relax for a moment. Then I took a deep breath and gave it all I had. "Tlll Buh en nnnn mmmr."

Matt spoke up. "Can I get Ben?"

"Yes," Slocum answered.

"Go on, Andy," Big Rich said as Matt returned with Ben and Joanne.

"Nnnn mmmmr!"

Ben knew immediately what I had been trying to say. He ran up to me, gave me Maggie's tight pixie-like smile. Then his eyes began watering up. Not wanting me to see him cry, Ben leaned over, put his cheek next to mine, buried his face in my pillow, and gently hugged me.

When I felt him shake, I said, "Yyy Buh . . . Yyy Buh . . . Yyy Buh en."

16 WHEN THE FIRST rays of Monday's sun entered my room, my ears were already straining for bits of local newscasts from the room with the radio.

Slocum brought news, too. "Your friends and that social worker are something else!" he exclaimed as he removed bandages, exposing my sweating cheek to the air of the room. "Last night I told the O'Briens it was okay for Ben to spend an hour a day with you if it were possible. Within minutes, some of your friends talked to Mr. Laveck and he had called the institution and received approval."

"Yyyyyy eh!"

"Thought you'd like that. Since Matt's on Christmas vacation, he'll do shuttle duty this week—pick up Ben at 5:00 and have him back at 9:30. Your son will be with you from 6:00 until 7:00—no longer.

"But that's this evening. Some speech and physical therapists and other specialists will come in and do evaluations today."

They came, all right. Six of them gathered around my bed, moved my limbs, checked my muscle tone, watched how high I could blow a ping-pong ball in a vertical plastic tube, and had me do exercises with my lips and tongue. I tried to do everything they told me, even though Ben's evening visit was uppermost in my mind.

At 6:00, Ben marched into the room, his arms swinging just as they used to. Matt and Slocum followed. When Ben approached my side, he halted like a soldier on parade, glanced at Slocum, then at me.

"You can touch your dad," Slocum said.

That was all Ben needed. He reached down with both hands and kneaded the muscles that connected my shoulders to my neck, as he had done hundreds of times when I came home tense and exhausted from my bus runs. It was one of his regular, no-big-deal tasks.

This time, however, his hands felt as if they were giving a cup of water to a person dying of thirst. His touch set off a carnival inside me, with confetti and waving flags and the music of a calliope and the smell of cotton candy and a sense of being free and wanting to laugh at the drop of a hat. Those wonderful, loving, healing hands! They soothed me and made me feel human again.

I thought about all the therapists who had been in my room earlier, trying to figure out where they should begin. Then Ben showed up and, in minutes, had made my ready-to-fall-apart body whole again.

"Feel good, Dad?"

"Yyyy Buh."

"Sure mmmissed ya, Dad."

"Mmmm yyy."

"Dad?"

"Yyy?"

"Sure glad you're not a hermmmit crab anymore."

"Yyyy uh!"

"Ben," Slocum said, coming over behind my son, "will you help your dad move the fingers of his right hand?"

"Mmmove his fingers?"

"Right." Slocum reached around and placed Ben's index finger in the palm of my hand. "Now you watch as your father tries to close his hand around it."

"Okaaay!" Ben said, looking at my hand as if a miracle were about to happen.

"Don't push him now. Just check him each time you visit."

"Yep."

"Barney's put some tables and chairs together at the far end of the diner," Matt said. "Mom and Dad, the Rooneys, and the Huffs are having a late dinner with Ben and me."

"Yyy."

"Then I'm going to drive Ben around town," Matt said. "He wants to check things out. You know—the town square, the high school, the compost heap at the house."

"Yep. Gotta check," Ben said.

I could tell that Matt wasn't just putting up with Ben, as he had in earlier days.

At 7:00, the boys left. Slocum had said I'd be tired by then. He wasn't kidding.

Tuesday, I was wheeled on a cart to the therapy department for move-your-lips-as-you-watch-in-the-mirror sessions. Then they propped me up, turned my head to the side, and told me to blow at a ping-pong ball on a table.

Wednesday, the same routine with a bright spot added. Heather Pendleton appeared as a volunteer and was assigned the ping-pong-ball-blowing exercises.

Thursday, Heather challenged me to blow harder. I did. That is, until I fainted. No problem. I came to and blew some more.

***

Of course, Ben and Matt showed up right at 7:00 each evening. Ben always greeted me by placing his index finger on my palm. "Go, Dad," he'd say. Then as I struggled to move my fingers, Ben would screw his face into a wrinkled frown—as if that would help me.

"Nuff, Dad," he'd say after awhile. "Try tomorrow." After Ben and Matt left they always carried out their diner-statue-school-compost heap routine.

At 6:55 on Thursday, Matt, Joanne, Big Rich, the Rooneys, the Huffs, and Polly all showed up. Each one gave me a pep talk. After they left for the diner, I pondered the concern they had shown this past week. Although my friends—and the professionals, too—had kept a noble silence about why they worked with me so intensely and rooted for me so much, I knew they were readying me for a crucial day—the day when I could confront Phoebe.

Although nobody told me about it that Thursday—I learned about it later—Matt had run into a problem at the institution. His daily right-on-time arrival had evidently made some of the ward attendants feel a tinge of jealousy. The ward supervisor, in an officious tone, had told Matt that Ben would soon be busy with his "individual habilitation plan." He'd have workshop assignments and education classes during the day and "structured recreation" in the evenings. Matt, sensing rightly that these happenings were many days away and that the ward staff members had become uncomfortable with his regular appearances, thanked the supervisor for telling him about it and said he'd do everything he could to cooperate.

As soon as the supervisor heard that, he had

made Matt feel like a member of the ward team. "You keep coming. We'll make sure Ben's ready."

But just to make sure everything was okay, after he drove off the grounds with Ben, Matt had stopped at a pay phone to call his mother. She passed the word to Fred Laveck, who volunteered to meet them at the diner.

"Matt handled it perfectly," Laveck had said. Then he explained how institutions tend to function like regiments—in spite of all the paperwork that calls for individual plans. He described "common-denominator rules," "institutional pecking orders," "interdepartmental jealousies and rivalries"—even "on-the-ward program sabotage"—that tend to infect such large residential settings.

"Institutions are far from familylike," Laveck had said. "Ward 3 in B Building, Ben's ward, houses 24 high-functioning teenagers, and even if we had the kindest people in the world on the staff, they would still be so overwhelmed by the myriad personal needs of these young people that they'd only have time and energy to *set limits* and *regiment* them as a group.

"The remarkable acceptance Ben received from his parents and sister—and from you people—we can never give."

Since Matt and Ben were due to arrive shortly, Laveck had been invited to stay at the diner for the regular meeting of the "Ben Banks Supper Club."

While they waited, Laveck shared more information, which excited the group so much that Manny had called Dr. Slocum. "Andy needs to hear this." Slocum, already at the hospital on an emergency, asked Laveck to come over, and at 9:15 they entered my room laughing.

"Well," Laveck began, "the superintendent called me in this afternoon and asked me what he ought to do about Benjamin Banks."

"Hhhuh?" I said.

"Seems that this feisty son of yours got tired of sitting around on the ward waiting for his 'individual habilitation plan' to be developed. He approached the supervisor and asked if he could rake up the leaves that were still on the ground. The superintendent checked with the ward, got clearance, gave Ben a rake and a pushcart, and told him to have at it." Laveck laughed. "That was a mistake. Ben raked so many leaves and made such a giant compost heap behind the institution that the regular workers . . . well, they're ashamed."

"Yyyy eh!" I said.

"They took Ben off that job and assigned him to work with a crew of men. But now there's another problem."

"Hhhuh?"

"Every time the crew takes a rest break, Ben storms into a ward, gives back rubs to nonambulatory residents, and teaches wrestling holes to the able-bodied ones. By the time the people on the staff gather their wits and tell him to leave, break time is over and he charges away like the Lone Ranger."

Even though every chuckle made my side feel as though it might rip open, I didn't care. I waited for more.

"At lunchtime, Ben scurries up and down the halls, pushing people in wheelchairs to the dining room—whether they need it or not."

"Hhha!" I said.

Laveck continued. "The grounds supervisor called the superintendent and *begged* him to finish Ben's rehabilitation plan soon."

"Sounds like your *institution* needs mercy now," Slocum said.

"Sure does," Laveck answered. "The superintendent is a career man with thirty years experience who's seen a lot of changes down through the years. He said, 'You know, Laveck, there was a day in this place when we took energetic people like that and slowed them down with drugs—or else we put them in straitjackets or locked them up in seclusion rooms.' "

Laveck became quiet for a moment. "Of

course, you have to understand, we're smarter now." He paused again.

"Mr. Banks," he went on, "the superintendent has ordered me to give top priority to getting Ben out of High Ridge and back to Seahaven. On Monday, I'm calling for an appointment with Mrs. Paxton and her lawyer in New York."

17 WHEN MY EYES opened Friday morning, the last day of the year, I automatically perked my ears for the sound of the radio. I heard nothing. During the night the occupant of that room had died.

Nobody had to tell me. I knew. A person spending time in a hospital bed learns quickly that every sound has meaning; patients often know more about what's going on than doctors and nurses ever dream.

I had liked that patient, even though I'd never met him. His love for the news had helped save me, even though it hadn't saved him.

That man's death helped me to realize that folks go to hospitals when they have health problems that medical people call *acute*. Something strikes or invades people—often with no warning and for no comprehensible reason. It messes up their flesh, jumbles up their body functions, and wrenches their brains. But most important, it pushes them toward a terrible turning point. After the turning point has been passed, they leave the hospital—some by one door, some by another. A chill came over me when I thought about Laveck's meeting with

Phoebe on Monday. It made me realize that my turning point was approaching.

At 10:00 my door swung open, banging against the doorstop. In walked Ben, Sarah, Matt, and Heather, all wearing winter parkas, gloves, blue jeans, and smiles. They lined up like a ski patrol reporting for duty.

Seeing Matt and Heather together made something clang inside me—something that didn't harmonize with my recollections of Matt and Beth. The dissonance faded, however, when I looked at Sarah. There she stood, a head shorter than Ben, bundled up like an Eskimo, the only one with her hood still up. Born two months after Ben, she had drawn the Rooneys and the Banks into a long-term friendship. Through the years, Sarah and Ben had been school chums, and because she and Ben had the same kind of eyes, we often had to tell people they were not brother and sister.

Ben reached over and gently pulled off her hood and smoothed her hair.

"Mr. Banks," Matt asked, "can Ben go with us to New York? We want to be in Times Square when the apple drops."

"Mr. Laveck worked it so Ben can stay with the O'Briens tonight," Heather added.

Ben tapped Heather on the arm and corrected her: "Tommorrow mmorning!" puffing out his chest.

"Ben can stay with us until Sunday evening," Matt said.

The four became silent. I made them wait for my answer.

"Yyy eh," I said when I felt they'd stood there long enough.

"Great!" Matt exclaimed, and in a few seconds they were gone.

As New Year's Eve drew near, activity at the hospital came to a near standstill. I chose to sleep away as much of it as I could. The more I rested, the more strength would flow into my system—so I thought.

***

Saturday morning, New Year's Day, Dr. Slocum said that many of my friends had been scheduled to visit me briefly at different times during the day. Joanne came first, showing up at 10:00.

"Those crazy kids are still dead to the world," she said. "When they came in this morning, they got us up for a blow-by-blow account of their trip.

"When they arrived at Grand Central Station, they checked out the large color photograph of a winter scene that covered the whole upper east wall.

"Then they visited the Statue of Liberty and took a round trip on the Staten Island Ferry.

"They had dinner at the Zum Zum Restaurant in the Pan Am Building. Ben and Sarah thought that any establishment with a name like Zum Zum had to be a glorious place to eat.

"At Rockefeller Center they watched the skaters on the rink, and then they stood around the security desk in the RCA Building, watching famous TV people come down from the studios.

"The movie they saw was only 'so-so.' When they got out it was almost midnight, and they pushed through the crowds in Times Square until they were right next to the statue of George M. Cohan. Then when everybody was blowing horns and cheering, Matt boosted Sarah and Ben up on the statue's pedestal. When the apple descended, there stood Ben on one side of George M., and Sarah on the other.

"When Ben tried to describe that sea of faces and the noise, he stretched out his arms as if he were trying to touch both walls of the room. A few seconds later he was fast asleep."

For the rest of the day, my friends opened their visits with their versions of the adventures of the Times Square Four. I never got tired of hearing about them.

On Sunday the schedule contained some time shifts, but the same folks visited. They didn't talk a lot, but I felt good, just knowing they were there.

Fred Laveck stopped on his way to New York, where he planned to stay overnight and be fresh for Monday's meeting with Phoebe.

When all the visiting ended, I closed my eyes and slipped into a deep sleep.

18   ON BIG MONDAY, I waited all morning for news of Laveck's meeting with Phoebe. But aside from people doing the routines, checking temperature, blood pressure, and all, nobody entered my room.

At noon, Slocum arrived. Without looking at my face, he put on his stethoscope and listened to my heart. While he checked the bandages, he still avoided eye contact.

"Tlll," I said.

Slocum didn't look up.

"Tllll!"

Slocum looked at me sadly.

"Tlllll uhh!"

"Can we talk later?" he said.

"Nnnnn!"

"Mr. Banks, Phoebe Paxton's lawyer and another man appeared unannounced at the High Ridge superintendent's office this morning. The lawyer presented affidavits signed by Mrs. Peck, stating that she had seen Ben in Seahaven every day. He ordered that Ben be discharged immediately.

"The other man was a Joe McGlone, a man with credentials for working with the mentally ill. McGlone and Ben are now en route to

LaGuardia Airport to board a flight for San Diego. Ben is being delivered to a private institution.

"Fred Laveck is on his way here," Slocum went on, "and he . . . Mr. Banks, can you hear me? . . . "

I heard him, all right, but I didn't respond. I was too busy counting the tiles on the ceiling.

19   THE SAME OLD nightmares came back, but I wasn't the same guy. When Phoebe smiled like a barracuda and began her biting preachments in perfect English, I yelled at her to shut up and get out. When other torturers appeared, I made it plain that I refused to be anybody's victim any longer.

***

I cracked my eyes and noticed the room was dim. Glancing toward the window, I saw it was dark outside.

"Fffingers, Dad."

I heard those soft, businesslike words and suddenly felt a pudgy, stubby index finger pressed against my palm. Opening my eyes wider, I saw Ben's face staring into mine—those strangely formed eyelids and the always-struggling tongue, the caring brown eyes of Beth, Maggie's smile, and those high cheek-bones.

"Fffingers, Dad."

Although I was puzzled by Ben's presence, I tried to get my brain ready to organize nerves, muscles, and digits, make them cooperate like members in an orchestra. I concentrated, took three deep breaths, and said Go! to myself. Then, using all the power I could muster, every movable part of my hand quivered until it closed around my son's finger.

Dr. Slocum said, "Ben, I think your dad is on his way."

20   HOW BEN had appeared at my side was something else! In the next few days, little groups of my friends gathered round me like excited children, each chiming in with what he or she had seen. They interrupted one another, repeated themselves, each jewel of information reinforced with Yeah and other such exclamations. After many recitals, I finally pieced it all together.

When word had come from High Ridge that McGlone and Ben were en route to LaGuardia, Dr. Slocum called Joanne O'Brien. She had contacted Big Rich just in time for him to find a substitute for his truck run. Then she called the Rooneys, the Huffs, and Polly Patterson. Polly had asked her assistant to take over while she, Sarah, and Josh ran to the principal's office to get Matt and Heather excused for the day. When Barney was called, he shut down his diner.

Forty-five minutes later, everyone had met at the statue on the town square. Quickly, they voted to retain a lawyer and split the bill. Polly hurried to the travel agency that faced the square and returned with the information that McGlone's American Airlines flight was scheduled to take off for San Diego at 7:12 P.M.. Nine people had piled into two cars. One headed for the city, while Manny, Polly, Barney, Laveck, and Dr. Slocum looked for an attorney. When one quickly agreed to take the case, Slocum returned to the hospital while the other four sped toward New York. Everybody had agreed to meet in front of the bust of Mayor LaGuardia in the airport lobby.

At 6:30, Ben and the towering McGlone, whose biceps stretched the sleeves of his sweatshirt, had appeared in the mass of humanity hurrying toward the security detectors just inside the concourse for American Airlines. As McGlone and Ben waited in line to place their suitcases on the conveyor belt and walk through the X-ray unit, Sarah and Josh had run toward them, shouting "Hi Ben! Hi Ben!" They threw their arms around Ben, hugging him as if he were a long-lost brother.

McGlone watched the kids greeting Ben, but didn't notice a number of pushy adults who had gathered around him, slowly moving him three yards away from Ben and his embracing friends.

Heather suddenly appeared. She pointed toward Joanne, who was standing at the entrance of the concourse, and told Ben to crouch down and run to her as fast as he could.

When Ben reached Joanne, she pointed down the connecting hall to Georgia Huff, who stood at the entrance of the next concourse. "Run to Georgia!" she yelled.

McGlone, seeing Ben take off, elbowed through the crowd like a wild man and charged after him, knocking people aside as he went.

As Ben approached the next concourse, Georgia pointed past the United ticket counters to Polly. "Run to Polly!" she called out and then stepped back, because McGlone was closing fast, ready to grab Ben's shoulders as he turned the corner.

But just as he reached out, there was a THUD, and McGlone flew backward through the air, arms and legs apart as if he'd been struck by a cannonball. He landed on his back, the wind knocked out of him.

Standing over him was Matt, a suitcase in his hand. "Are you all right, Sir?" Matt asked. "I'm so sorry, Sir. I'm late for my plane and I didn't see you coming around the corner."

McGlone didn't answer. His hands clutched his belly where Matt's shoulder had made solid contact.

"I'm sorry, Sir," Matt said again. "Hope you'll be okay. Gotta run."

In the meantime, Ben had reached Polly at the far end of the ticket counter. Hand in hand, they doubled-stepped down the escalator and ran through the baggage pickup area. Out the door, they dived into Sally Rooney's car and disappeared in traffic.

***

Of course, Ben's first stop after his escape was the hospital. And when everybody finally convinced me to release Ben's finger, he went home with the O'Briens and to bed.

The next morning at 10:00, with everybody assembled at the O'Briens, Ben left the house, checked his compost heap, then walked over to Mrs. Peck's.

"Hi, Mmmrs. Peck," Ben said when she answered the door.

"What? . . . Why hello, Ben," she said. "Uh . . . What are you doing here?"

"I'mm back. Wanted to say hello."

"Wha . . . Why, yes. Hello."

Ben waved good-bye and went back to the O'Briens.

Thirty minutes later, Phoebe Paxton and Lawyer Battersby stormed into the O'Brien residence, both shouting threats and spouting the law—that is, until they spied another lawyer sitting in an easy chair, with a pile of documents on his lap and all my friends standing behind him.

A few minutes later, they silently walked out of the O'Brien house, got in their car, and drove away.

21 "THAT GANG OF YOURS!"

Dr. Slocum remarked as he came in my room. "Wanting to celebrate the last day of Mardi Gras!"

"You wouldn't let them celebrate Valentine's Day, " I reminded him, still feeling a little rubberiness at the side of my mouth where a trace of paralysis lingered.

Slocum looked at me as I sat fully dressed in a wheelchair.

"You weren't ready then. Do you feel ready now?"

"Sure do."

"I think you are. They tell me you've been a tiger in therapy these past six weeks." Slocum smiled. "Besides, this hospital needs a respite from Ben. Just think! Tonight, no people in wheelchairs will be pushed against their will. Paid staff members will have to move the supper carts themselves, and nobody will smuggle dogs, worms, or soil samples into your room."

"Sounds as if you'll be glad to get me out of here," I said.

Slocum walked to the window and stared at

the oak limb. "You know," he said, "during the holidays, I expected you to leave this place through the back door in a body bag."

"I was some case, huh?"

"You were. We couldn't get a handle on all the injuries."

"Look, Doc," I said, "I'm quite a bluff. There's a lot I'm not over yet."

"I know. But you have more to live for than most."

***

Big Rich and Joanne drove me to the high school where the Seahaven Dolphins were playing the Havenville Sharks. It was the final game of the season.

"We'll take you in early and have you settled before the other fans arrive," Big Rich said.

"Wait'll you see what Auggy and Manny did," Joanne said. "They've built you a special chair with armrests and a back; it attaches onto the front bleacher seat."

When they wheeled me in, my friends were already there, sitting to the left of the hometown bench. They rose to their feet and cheered as if I had been a player.

"C'mon, you guys. Keep it down," I said, even though I enjoyed the reception.

"We've got this throne for you." Auggy pointed.

"Looks pretty cushy," I said.

"Planned it that way," Manny said. "C'mon guys, let's get him into it."

"Have we got a surprise for you!" Polly said behind me.

"Polly," I answered, "I've had enough surprises for a lifetime."

I waved and spoke to Sarah and Josh, sitting three rows back. "Didn't know you kids were basketball fans."

"They've been great fans," Heather said, "ever since Ben came back and began helping Matt."

"Hey, Barney," I called, "don't tell me the diner's closed down again."

"Just for the game, Andy."

"Can't make a living doing that."

"Well, Mr. Laveck here said he'd take over for me," Barney joked. "But turning it over to a social worker would have been the kiss of death for my business."

Everybody laughed.

As others filtered into the gym, I sat back, watched, and breathed easy. Then out of the corner of my eye, I noticed Brill on duty at the far exit, looking at me. When I stared back, he casually lifted his head, stood ramrod straight, and began to listen for messages from outer space again. I hated that guy. But I feared him, too, for what he could do to Ben.

A flood of purple-and-white-uniformed Seahaven players poured onto one end of the court, followed by Matt and Ben, both wearing managers' jackets and carrying armloads of equipment. Havenville's flood of crimson and gold entered at the other end. The crowd let out a deafening roar. I cheered, too—for Ben.

After unloading equipment on the bench, Matt picked up a clipboard and stood next to the coach. Ben dragged a large bag onto the court and, like an automatic machine, cannoned practice balls to the players. That done, he whirled around and lined up the water container, a stack of towels, a first-aid kit, and two boxes of equipment on the end of the bench, placing everything just so.

When the buzzer sounded, Ben moved like a high-speed vacuum cleaner, picking up balls and putting them into the bag. Then he slung the bag over his shoulder and hustled for the locker room. He whizzed by me, eyes front, serious business written all over his face.

"Hey Ben!" Manny shouted.

Ben only ran faster.

When he returned, he plopped down on the bench next to Matt.

I was so taken by Ben's expertise that I ignored the beginning of the game and turned to Polly. "Holy mackerel!" I said. "How'd he learn to do all that?"

"When Ben came back to stay with the O'Briens," she explained, leaning forward, "he spent time on the bleachers watching Matt. And . . . well, you know me. I helped Coach Rossi make a list of the team manager's duties. Then we showed Matt how to teach Ben to do some of them and how to reinforce him when he did them perfectly."

"Didn't Matt resent it?"

"Nope. Every time Ben took over a task, the coach gave Matt a new assignment. Now Matt stays at the coach's side, charting shots, computing percentages, writing down future strategies the coach dictates from time to time, and just helping out generally."

Just then a Seahaven player received an elbow in the eye and time-out was called. Ben quickly grabbed a clean towel and positioned himself behind the coach. When Rossi asked for the towel, Ben slapped it to him before the man had finished the sentence.

A few minutes later I noticed Ben leaning over Matt's clipboard. "Looks like my kid is hedging into more of Matt's territory," I said to Polly.

"He's learned to call out the shooting player's number and tell Matt where he shot from. Don't worry, your son won't take over the computations." She smiled. "At least not this year."

By the middle of the fourth quarter, Seahaven was trailing 58 to 70. I couldn't have cared less. That is, until it hit me that I was beaming while everybody else looked glum. So I put on an anxious face, too. When the coach called a time-out, the players gathered around him, agony in their eyes. Ben moved into the circle and passed out towels like a Samaritan. Then as he gathered the towels, he gave each player a pat, not saying a word.

For the next six or seven minutes, the Seahaven players rallied. But again, you couldn't have proved it by me. I was back to watching that assistant manager, bouncing nervously on the bench.

When the Havenville team called another time-out with 15 seconds to go, I did unhook from Ben long enough to notice that the score was tied 74 to 74. Everyone had come off the Seahaven bench, crowding around the five, telling them to go for it. And my son was scrunched in their midst, his hands reaching out to every player.

After the action resumed, Seahaven swished the ball through the net just as the final buzzer sounded, winning the game.

Ben jumped up, raced onto the floor, and was the first to congratulate the Seahaven five. And each player grabbed Ben and hugged him, lifting him off the floor—treating him like a "regular."

Afterward, Barney suggested a stopover at the diner. "Got this juicy burger-with-the-works waiting for you," he said. The rest decided to stop, too. So off we went, Ben pushing me in the wheelchair, hovering over me like Punjab over Little Orphan Annie.

At the diner, everyone fell into a pensive mood, eating quietly and saying little.

"You know," Laveck said, "I try to tell others at High Ridge about you people, and I can't put it into words."

"Don't need to," Ben said. He put his fork down and sat upright, hands on hips. "Just remmemmber to never give up."

Ben picked up his fork and was at work on his pie again when Officer Brill came in. He spied us at the end of the otherwise empty diner and took a stool at the opposite end.

Barney walked over and served him.

My mouth became dry and my muscles tightened. Brill was the last person I wanted to be in the same room with me. Everyone grew silent.

Ben looked at me for a minute, then studied the faces of the others. He put down his fork and stepped briskly toward Brill. He tapped Brill on the shoulder, snapping him out of his usual trance.

"Hi, Officer Brill," Ben said. "Remmemmber me? *Ben*."

"Oh . . . yeah . . . Ben."

"Great game, huh?"

"Yeah, Ben. Great game."

EPILOGUE

"Move that rake!" I said.

"Mmove your own," came the reply.

Working side by side, Ben and I pulled the leaves toward our feet as music from a portable radio provided rhythm for our strokes.

It was the Saturday before Thanksgiving; I had a day off from my bus run, and since the sun was shining and a warm breeze had whisked in off the ocean, Ben and I decided to have a go at the leaves.

Tillie was bellied-down on the ground beside the compost enclosure and looked like a large-eyed little supervisor, scrutinizing every move we made.

Dr. Slocum said I'd made remarkable recovery from the physical injuries of a year ago. I agreed, but I didn't tell him about certain aches on rainy days. As for the psychological injuries Ben and I had experienced, that was another thing. Even so, the two of us were working hard to make a new life.

"Couldn't have a better day," I said.

"Yep," Ben answered without looking up, making sure his strokes kept up with mine as we worked.

The tune coming over the radio ended.

"There you have it, folks. The number 3 song on this week's chart.

"And now, Bosworth's Quality Meats wants to remind you that friends and loved ones will gather together for Thanksgiving. And on that, one of the happiest, most meaningful days of the year—"

Ben threw his rake down and ran for the house. Tillie jumped up and streaked after him, just making it inside before the screen door slammed. A few seconds later, noises from Ben's CB came from his room.

I left him alone, knowing that both of us had a rough day coming. Ben and I had weekly sessions with Fred Laveck as he helped us pull out of things. He said holidays would be the toughest times.

Our friends understood. They tried not to mention the word *Thanksgiving* around us—but they had *ordered* us to spend the day with them at the O'Briens and to play cards until bedtime.

Matt will be home from college, where he's a promising freshman on the football team. He told his folks he was considering a major in special education. He wanted to talk to Polly about it when he got home.

I can predict Polly's enthusiasm when she describes her new program: "peer-group" education—in which regular students take special training from her and then help out in one-to-one, in-class teaching of her students— and receive academic credit for their efforts, too.

Fred Laveck will be there. Ever since he was playfully voted in as a member-in-good-standing of the old Ben Banks Supper Club, he has been to many of our get-togethers. He even gave a talk to our parent group.

The Rooneys and the Huffs had volunteered to come early and help with the cooking; so Sarah and Josh will probably come over, sit cross-legged with Ben in his room, and share one more account of saving Ben from San Diego.

Although Heather will have dinner with her own family, she had said she'd come over later. These last few months she has become a real pal to Ben and me, dropping in every now and then. The day I started to take Maggie's clothes out of the closet, she came to help. She helped gather up things in Beth's room, too. She stuck right with me. It was her suggestion that made me leave Beth's guitar on the bed, along with the penciled notes to her song. Everybody calls it "Beth's Song" now.

Before Matt left for college, he'd taken a shine to Heather. Now that he's been away, I hope all those college lovelies haven't taken his mind off her.

Phoebe called this morning, as if nothing had ever happened. In her usual high-pitched voice, she told us not to worry about her for Thanksgiving and mentioned the names of some high-born sounding persons who had magnanimously invited her to dinner. She had ended our conversation by asking me to give her best regards to "dear, sweet Mrs. Peck and that helpful Officer Brill."

I didn't tell her that Mrs. Peck hadn't been her usual self this summer. When Ben tried to give her tomatoes, she had responded that she didn't like tomatoes because they gave her heartburn—but would like some of his cucumbers.

As for Brill, he ignores Ben now—except when the little charger breaks through the cop's facade with a bubbly "Hello there Officer Brill." Then Brill responds by calling him "kid" instead of "Ben." My hate for the guy began to cool when it dawned on me that some people are doomed to die with their prejudices.

When we sit down to dinner Thursday, Ben will insist on wearing his purple jacket with the large white chenille S on it, and I'll insist he take it off. (Coach Rossi gave him a letter and asked him to help manage the team again this year.)

Later in the day Ben, Matt, Sarah, Josh, and Heather will become bored when the rest of us begin to shuffle cards. Then Ben will probably suggest that they take Matt to see the new tennis courts at Seahaven High—the ones laid out where Polly's old annex building used to be before her students were transferred to a room in the main building.

When they've finished at the school, Ben will lead them to the town square, where he'll deliver his—say 10,001st—object lesson on James Franklin Bannister.

So Thursday will be rough, all right, but Ben and I will be with our friends—a trucker, two professors, a diner operator, two housewives, a carpenter, and a social worker. And then there's a college athlete, a high school computer wizard, and two kids in special ed. We are all so different.

And yet when trouble came, we were united. In spite of our differences, we have a lot in common. We all seem to be able to admit that we're . . . well, not quite as perfect as we'd like to be . . . not quite finished.

That thought sets me wondering. Now, I'm no philosopher, but is it possible that deep inside every person there is the longing to be finished—a final edition—and when we discover we aren't and never will be, it hurts?

And maybe, when we refuse to face this single painful fact, we work overtime trying to prove to others that we *have* arrived? Maybe we work so hard at keeping up the bluff, we never notice we've developed inflexible, sharp edges which cut others who get too close?—and we even try to shove aside others whose unfinished natures are more apparent? Maybe—just maybe—that's why the Bens-of-the-world sometimes are ignored and held back, though they have done nothing to deserve such treatment.

I began to rake alone. Then I noticed Ben's rake moving, keeping up with mine again.

I glanced at the straight line of leaves and noticed that Ben was pulling faster. I picked up speed, too.

"Think you can do better than me?" I said.

Both rakes flashed as if they were attached to machines going full throttle.

THE END